My Jesus
Loves Gays

My Jesus Loves Gays

WHY BIBLE-BELIEVING CHRISTIANS
SHOULD LOVE AND ACCEPT
LGBTQ PEOPLE

ROBERT WILLIAMS

Fairholme Press
ISBN-9781798844342

Unless otherwise noted, all Scripture quotations are from
the New International Version (NIV) of the Bible.

To my kids
Loved by Jesus.

Contents

Introduction

It's a Friday night and our house is bursting with energetic teenagers, two of our own and five of their friends. They are a colorful and animated group, talking too loudly all at once for me to follow any of their conversations.

And they are all gay.

My office is our old dining room, so my desk is right in the middle of all of this adolescent ruckus.

Violet, a tall trans girl with high cheek bones, wanders over to my desk. She sees the Bible app open on one of my computer screens and the draft of Sunday's sermon on the other, and asks cautiously, "You're a pastor, right?"

I grin at how out of place this question feels. "Yeah," I answer.

She gestures around the room at all these teens in a grandiose wave of inclusion. "You have gay kids, and your house is full of gay teens." There is a pause as if she's trying to figure out what question she wants to ask. "How does that work?"

It's a fair question, one I've been asking myself for a long time. How does a Bible-believing pastor of an evangelical church host a gaggle of gay teens, creating a space in his own home that is considered safe and non-judgmental?

It took me a minute, but eventually I replied, slowly and deliberately, as if this summarized everything, "My Jesus loves gays."

He really does.

So do I.

This book is an explanation of that answer. My hope is that more people who follow Jesus will do the same: love LGBTQ people and show that love by opening up their lives, homes, and even churches to be places of loving inclusion.

1

Red, Not Scarlet, Letters

My own journey to a place of love and acceptance involved a change of both heart and mind. I was raised in a culture that condemned LGBTQ individuals, forcing them to live closeted and secret lives. Despite attending public schools in a liberal American city, none of my classmates or teachers were openly gay. No one in my family or church was gay. No one spoke of any gay relatives. I was forced to confront my own beliefs, prejudices, and attitudes only after close LGBTQ loved ones finally confided in me. They had been there all along. Now that the truth was out I had to choose whether to accept those whom I loved.

To my surprise, the way forward toward accepting love was not abandoning my faith, but instead focusing more intently on the heart of my faith: Jesus and his mission. While I may feel at odds with certain members of my church and oppose the current stance of my denomination, I believe that my theology lines up with the teaching of Jesus. My desire is that my actions follow my convictions so that the LGBTQ people I continue to meet encounter in me the Jesus who loves them.

My Exam

After years of schooling and internships, the final step to becoming a pastor in my denomination is a thorough examination by a large group of pastors and elders. During this exam, which lasts several hours, a candidate is expected to answer questions about their personal faith, lifestyle, the church, the Bible, and theology. Anything at all having to do with pastoral work is fair game.

One of the questions I was asked at my exam was, "Tell us your views on the red-letter edition of the Bible." This is an edition of the Bible which has the words of Jesus in red letters, while the rest of the Bible is printed in black letters.

I blurted out the first thing that came to mind. "It's really hard to read in dim lighting."

They laughed.

It's true, but not quite the truth they were looking for.

All joking aside, if you want to become a pastor you do have to eventually produce the right answer, the expected answer. So I went on to explain that the red letters were artificial, that the Bible wasn't originally written with the words of Jesus in a different colored ink. We are adding our interpretation to the text by using red letters.

This "red-letter interpretation" implies that the red-letter words of Jesus stand above his black-letter actions. This is a problem because we believe that Jesus, unlike the rest of us, was a person of perfect integrity: his words and actions line up completely. This means that we can learn as much from Jesus' actions as we do from his words; his black letters and red letters hold equal value.

Consider this example from Matthew 8:

> "When Jesus came down from the mountainside, large crowds followed him. A man with leprosy came and knelt before him and said, 'Lord, if you are willing, you can make me clean.' Jesus reached out his hand and touched the man. 'I am willing,' he said. 'Be clean!' Immediately he was cleansed of his leprosy. Then Jesus said to him, 'See that you don't tell anyone. But go, show yourself to the priest and offer the gift Moses commanded, as a testimony to them." (Matthew 8:1-4)

We learn as much from Jesus touching the leper as we do from the words he spoke to the leper, maybe even more. No one touched lepers. It was forbidden. It violated the religious laws and customs. Yet Jesus touched the man. With his actions Jesus taught that some rules, some historic traditions, even some religious laws, needed to be broken in order to show love for the outcast.

I also mentioned in my exam that the red letters seem to indicate that Jesus' words are more "the Word of God" than the rest of the Bible, that his words are more important, more true than the Old Testament prophets or the letters of the Apostle Paul.

That idea seems to contradict 2 Timothy 3:16-17, which I smartly quoted in my answer during the exam:

> "All Scripture is God-breathed and is useful for teaching, rebuking, correcting and training in righteousness, so that all God's people may be thoroughly equipped for every good work." (2 Timothy 3:16-17)

All Scripture is God's word, the entire Bible, not just the red letters of Jesus.

That was my answer several decades ago. To summarize: The red-letter version implies that the words of Jesus are more important than his actions, and that his spoken word is more the word of God than the rest of the Bible; therefore, it is not a good thing to add red ink to an otherwise black-lettered Bible. I told them that I wasn't about to throw out my Bible just because it has red letters, but that we all need to beware of these two potential errors when reading a red-letter edition of the Bible.

The group liked my answer. It was what they wanted to hear. They approved me, ordained me, and I've been a pastor ever since.

The Final Word

But these days I'm not so sure my answer was completely right.

I wonder if the red letters of Jesus really are more important than, say, the black letters of Moses or Ezekiel.

The Bible itself seems to teach that. This is how the New Testament book of Hebrews begins:

"In the past God spoke to our ancestors through the prophets at many times and in various ways, but in these last days he has spoken to us by his Son, whom he appointed heir of all things, and through whom also he made the universe. The Son is the radiance of God's glory and the exact representation of his being, sustaining all things by his powerful word. After he had provided purification for sins, he sat down at the right hand of the Majesty in heaven. So he became as much superior to the angels as the name he has inherited is superior to theirs." (Hebrews 1:1-4)

The argument being made here is simply that Jesus is superior to all, the name above all names. As great as Moses was, he was not "the exact representation of God's being." King David was great, but not "appointed heir of all things." Jeremiah's words might have been powerful, but Jesus "sustains all things by his powerful word." The point is that Jesus is superior to all messengers, prophets, and even the angels themselves.

And, yes, God spoke in the past through prophets like Isaiah and Ezekiel, and even through angels from time to time, but there is no word more powerful, more true, more God's own word, than the very words of Jesus, those red-lettered words.

The words of Jesus on a given subject are superior to all others. Should there be some real or perceived difference between Moses and Jesus, or anyone else and Jesus, Jesus is the final word. He gets the final say because his words stand above all others.

This shouldn't shock Christians.

The Christian faith is based on the person of Jesus. His life, death, and resurrection are the basis for our religion. Jesus is the center of our faith and the center of the Bible's revelation. Paul says that his preaching and ministry was simply "Jesus Christ and him crucified" (1 Corinthians 2:2). The best summary of the Christian life is that Jesus is Lord. Everything in the Christian life focuses on him.

Jesus is the main character of the Bible; it tells his story. Not just the four gospels either. The entire Old Testament points to the arrival of Jesus as Messiah. The rest of the Bible, the New Testament, fleshes out the story of Jesus, explaining the difference that faith in Jesus makes in the lives of believers and in the community of the church. The entire Bible is either back story to Jesus or pointing back to Jesus.

You could make a case, then, that those red letters are more vital to our faith than many of the black letters, that the words of Jesus really do stand above all other words.

Because Jesus is the main character of the Bible, we read everything else in the Bible in light of Jesus, through the eyes of Jesus, through the life of Jesus. His red-letter words and black-letter actions clarify everything before and color everything after. He is the center of our faith.

John, the poet disciple, hints at this at the beginning of his account of the life of Jesus:

> "In the beginning was the Word, and the Word was with God, and the Word was God. He was with God in the beginning. Through him all things were made; without him nothing was made that has been made. In him was life, and that life was the light of all people." (John 1:1-4)

It's not just that Jesus' words are above all others. He is the Word! At the beginning of everything when there was a big bang of creation energy, when God said "Let there be light," it was the voice of Jesus that could be heard in the ever-expanding universe, the Word that was God.

John continues to explain:

> "The Word became flesh and made his dwelling among us. We have seen his glory, the glory of the one and only Son, who came from the Father, full of grace and truth." (John 1:14)

Christians believe that God became flesh in the person of Jesus, thus Jesus' words were the precise words of our creator God. Jesus is the very word of God, not as a vague concept, but as a flesh and blood person whose words we can hear and actions we can see. Jesus, most perfectly, makes God known.

It seems to me that John's description, along with Hebrews 1, does elevate the words of Jesus to some red-letter status, words that define all other words, even those in other parts of the Bible. Maybe I should have failed my exam after all.

So what difference does that make in how we understand homosexuality, how we respond to LGBTQ people?

All the difference in the world.

2

All The Red Letters That Address Homosexuality

[This page intentionally blank]

N ot a word.

Jesus never specifically addressed homosexuality.

That fact reveals something about his own attitudes toward humanity, regardless of their sexual identity or orientation.

Given that the Lord of the church is silent on the subject, it is puzzling that so many churches, so many pastors and church leaders, have focused on this issue while ignoring so much of what Jesus did directly address—sins like pride, being judgmental, gossip, greed, and especially hypocrisy.

While Jesus doesn't directly address homosexuality, there is a lot we can learn from his words and actions (his red and black letters) about how he views and treats LGBTQ people.

The love and acceptance he offers to all does not exclude LGBTQ people. As the creative voice of the universe, Jesus is not surprised that some people are born gay or transgender. And he loves them along with the rest of humanity. Those of us who follow Jesus and want to be faithful to his values and mission may need to rethink our condemnation of those whom our Lord accepts. We should watch Jesus closely and learn from him how to love those scorned by society, how to display God's unconditional love through our own acts of loving acceptance. We cannot claim to follow Jesus if we refuse to love as he loved, if we ignore the kindness Jesus offered to everyone he encountered.

3

What Would Jesus Say To Freddy Mercury?

Suppose, in 1984, the flamboyant lead singer of the rock group *Queen*, Freddy Mercury, is leaving a concert and stumbles across Jesus. What do you think Jesus would say to him? Would he lecture Freddy on his poor moral choices or would he embrace him as a fellow child refugee? Would he condemn him as a homosexual or love him as a child of God?

While Jesus never specifically addresses homosexuality in any of his teaching, we do get a clear enough picture of Jesus through his words and actions recorded in the gospels that we can answer this question with certainty.

He Touched The Outcast

Consider again the encounter between Jesus and the man with leprosy, as told in Matthew 8:1-4. I recently visited a leper colony in southern India where over a hundred men and women stricken with leprosy huddled together on cheap plastic chairs in the shade of a large canopy to share their stories.

One by one they told sad tales of social rejection and the toll it took on their souls. Because of the disease and the resulting disfiguration, these lepers are feared. No one wants them around. A middle-aged man in a tattered sport coat explained how his family asked him to leave the very day he was diagnosed with leprosy. His disease brought a dark cloud of shame and suspicion on his family. No one

9

would visit a family housing a leper or invite such a family to any social gathering. His employer could not have a leper helping customers, handling merchandise, or even lingering on the premises. Cast out from family, friends, and co-workers, this man had no choice but to join the band of lepers living at the edge of the city in a ramshackle colony.

Leviticus 13, a book of laws in the Old Testament, teaches God's people how to treat leprosy. It is remarkably similar to how they are treated in India today. Leviticus says that leprosy makes a person unclean, unfit to mingle with others. Such unclean people with infectious diseases should not be touched by godly people. Touching such an unclean person makes the clean person unclean, even if they accidentally bump into each other (Leviticus 5:3). Lepers in ancient Israel and in Jesus' day had to cover themselves, call out "unclean," and stay far away from all non-lepers. Leviticus teaches that it is a sin to touch a leper.

So did Jesus sin when touched the leper?

Only if you believe that the laws of Leviticus are binding for all people in all times and places. Only if you consider the Pharisee's judgment of Jesus as "a friend of sinners" as a condemnation instead of a compliment.

But if you believe the words of Jesus spoken just before this encounter with the leper, then you understand how his actions speak consistently with his words in defining this as an act of righteousness. Here's what Jesus said in the Sermon on the Mount:

> "Do not think that I have come to abolish the Law or
> the Prophets; I have not come to abolish them but to
> fulfill them." (Matthew 5:9)

Again, the words and actions of Jesus always align; his red and black letters agree completely. His actions in touching the untouchable begin to teach what fulfilling the law is all about.

The miraculous transaction of the encounter between Jesus and the leper is that, instead of Jesus becoming spiritually unclean or physically diseased, the leper becomes clean and is healed completely of his disease. The flow of spiritual contagion is reversed in Jesus. Where sin once spread like a nasty virus, now righteousness spreads like blooming flowers of spring. The old law is fulfilled in the embrace of love between Jesus and the leper.

Jesus doesn't abolish religion (he instructed this newly healed man to go show himself to the priest, a necessary step in his restoration and a testimony to Jesus as Christ), or toss out the scriptures that we refer to as the Old Testament, but he redefines them. From now on an accurate reading of the Old Testament can only be done through the life of Jesus.

Today's Untouchables

Most gay people can identify with lepers: untouchable, spoken about in hushed whispers, judged and condemned, too often asked to leave their families and alienated from friends. The comedian Ellen DeGeneres, in her Netflix show *Relatable,* notes that side effects of being gay, "may include: loss of family, loss of friends, unemployment." She goes on to tell her story of emotional pain that is remarkably similar to that of the lepers I met in India.

Just as touching a leper made a person unclean, a suspect for having the disease, being too close, too friendly, or speaking up too much for the rights of LGBTQ people can have the same effect today.

That should not stop us.

Despite the social pressure and the religious forbiddance, Jesus touched the most untouchable person in that society. That same Jesus offers his touch of acceptance and words of healing to anyone who reaches out to him today.

I am convinced that Jesus would wrap Freddy Mercury in an embrace of love, not slap him with more guilt. Jesus always seemed to attract the most public of sinners, the written off and rejected. Without exception he accepted them with the open arms of grace. LGBTQ people are no more or no less a sinner than I am, and we all need that healing embrace which Jesus offers to all without discrimination.

When I shook a leper's hand, hugged another, placed my hands on another's shoulders as we prayed together, I was doing what Christians are suppose to do, imitating Jesus. And when I welcome gay teens into my home or have dinner with a gay couple, I am also imitating Jesus. If, in the process, I am accused of being a friend of sinners, I am in good company.

He Came for the Sick, Not the Healthy

Jesus' ministry targeted those whom society labeled as sinners. Tax collectors were as despised as any social group in those days. They were traitors, mercenaries, and cheats. Jesus shocked everyone by calling one of them to be his disciple. When Matthew accepted that call he immediately invited all of his friends to a celebration with Jesus, his new teacher and friend.

> "While Jesus was having dinner at Matthew's house, many tax collectors and sinners came and ate with him and his disciples. When the Pharisees saw this, they asked his disciples, 'Why does your teacher eat with tax collectors and sinners?'
>
> On hearing this, Jesus said, "It is not the healthy who need a doctor, but the sick. But go and learn what this means: 'I desire mercy, not sacrifice.' For I have not come to call the righteous, but sinners." (Matthew 9:10-13)

In a few sentences Jesus dismantles the old way of relating to God. Instead of an elaborate series of sacrifices, Jesus and his way of representing God is to offer mercy to sinners, to heal the spiritually sick with a healthy dose of accepting love.

Jesus is not opposed to righteous people. He does, however, oppose religion that creates barriers between groups of people, religion where the elite smugly call themselves "the Righteous" and write off the rest of humanity as "sinners." This is the opposite of Jesus' mission.

Such categories are simply meaningless to Jesus. Those who call themselves saints because of their sacrificial good deeds are, in actuality, no less sinners than those who have surrendered their wills to evil. In the eyes of Jesus everyone is a sinner and therefore everyone is in need of the mercy he offers equally to all sinners. The moral playing field is a level one and, without Jesus, it is a bog of spiritual despair.

Creating a separate category of sinner for LGBTQ people is simply wrong and might explain why Jesus never addressed homosexuality. There is no need to single out one type of sinner because Jesus loves us all, offers forgiveness for all our moral failures, and welcomes all the spiritually sick to an abundant life where sinners are redefined as saints.

He Offers an Easy Yoke

Jesus' view of humanity and his blanket offer of mercy to all sinners was, and is still, a stark contrast to the teachings of other religious leaders. In Jesus' day the specific teachings of a given Rabbi, the way in which they interpreted the law and applied it to life, was called a "yoke," like the tool used to harness an animal for pulling a load or plowing a field. The law, regardless of interpretation, was considered a burden, a yoke hung around a person's neck.

To those weighed down by religious rules and judgmental neighbors, Jesus says:

> "Come to me, all you who are weary and burdened, and I will give you rest. Take my yoke upon you and learn from me, for I am gentle and humble in heart, and you will find rest for your souls. For my yoke is easy and my burden is light." (Matthew 11:28-30)

While the contemporaries of Jesus were inventing new rules, weighing down their followers with the burden of laws that they could not keep, Jesus offers soul rest and inner peace. He offers himself, and those who accept his mercy will find the easy yoke of grace and the light burden of love.

Is Jesus not speaking directly to the Freddy Mercury's of the world?

Is he not offering his gentle self to those ostracized by a culture that condemns people based on their sexual identity?

Christians—those who represent Jesus today—should be welcoming LGBTQ people into their churches, churches that are communities of mercy where rest is offered for weary souls, where believers walk with Jesus together, gay and straight, and learn from his gentle, humble heart.

He Taught A Single Command

Part of Jesus easing the heavy burden on his followers was reducing the law, the entire moral code of human interaction, to the singular idea of love. Jesus takes not only the Ten Commandments but the hundreds of other commandments in the Old Testament; for that matter: all the rules, rituals, and commands of every world religion; and boils it down to one simple command:

> "A new command I give you: Love one another. As I have loved you, so you must love one another. By this everyone will know that you are my disciples, if you love one another." (John 13:34-35)

Love is the heart of following Jesus. It overrides all other commandments. If a particular verse in the Bible is applied in a non-loving manner, then it is being misunderstood or misused. Any verse or idea that we derive from the Bible must be filtered through Jesus' clear command to love one another.

Love is the final word on how we are to treat other people.

Not just any love, Jesus calls his followers to love "as I have loved you." This is sacrificial love, generous love that accepts the unacceptable and creates worth in those deemed worthless. It is love that never turns away the needy, love that serves others, love that gives until it hurts. It is the love we all need, and the love we all need to give.

4

Jesus is No Stoner

Jesus offered his sacrificial love to everyone he met. He extended love to powerful men and homeless women, Jews and Gentiles, adults and children. He loved with an unconditional, generous love that drew crowds of people who would never have darkened the door of a temple or synagogue.

That doesn't mean that Jesus condoned sinful lifestyles. Instead, by loving sinners, he called those he encountered into lives that honored God and were whole and healthy. This included their sexuality.

The Bible has a lot to say about sex. To simplify: Good sex is good for both people; it blesses body and soul. Whereas bad sex does the opposite and harms one or both parties; it belittles the sacred nature of human sexuality. The Bible reveals that God's design for good sex is that it is expressed in the emotional safe harbor of the permanent relationship of marriage.

Leviticus, in particular, has some teaching that sounds pretty harsh today, but was revolutionary in the ancient world with its "might makes right" mentality. Here's an example:

> "If a man commits adultery with another man's wife—
> with the wife of his neighbor— both the adulterer and
> the adulteress must be put to death." (Leviticus 20:10)

In the ancient world where women were considered property and lived with few if any legal protections, this law holds men culpable and creates gender equality in the punishment. If we followed this law from the Bible in our churches and in our country today there would be a lot more dead people. We don't, but it is Old Testament law and it was revered in Jesus' day as the authoritative teaching on adultery.

That's Law, now here's Gospel.

Jesus Doesn't Condemn

John records this story in the eighth chapter of his gospel:

> "The teachers of the law and the Pharisees brought in a woman caught in adultery. They made her stand before the group and said to Jesus, 'Teacher, this woman was caught in the act of adultery. In the Law Moses commanded us to stone such women. Now what do you say?' They were using this question as a trap, in order to have a basis for accusing him." (John 8:3-6)

This is classic trap: If Jesus says, "Stone her," then his message of love and grace means nothing; if he says, "Let her go," then he is denying God's law and proving that he, Jesus, is soft on sin. How can he represent a holy God if he approves of such unholy behavior?

We shouldn't ignore the fact that the adulterous man was nowhere to be seen, that the blatant sexism of that culture allowed him to stand above the law while this poor woman is cowering in her nighty in front of these arrogant men. We have always been good at elevating some sins above others, condemning some while letting others go.

> "But Jesus bent down and started to write on the ground with his finger. When they kept on questioning him, he straightened up and said to them, 'Let any one of you who is without sin be the first to throw a stone at her.' Again he stooped down and wrote on the ground." (John 8:6-8)

That's one of Jesus' most famous lines. Lots of people quote it to combat self-righteousness and may not even know that Jesus was the author of that statement.

We can only guess at what Jesus was writing on the ground. What is clear is that he is redefining morality, re-calibrating the moral compass of humanity away from harsh laws, toward the gracious offer of God's love. The very fingers that once wrote the Ten Commandments on stone are re-imagining the law in soft dirt.

> "At this, those who heard began to go away one at a time, the older ones first, until only Jesus was left, with the woman still standing there.
> Jesus straightened up and asked her, 'Woman, where are they? Has no one condemned you?'
> 'No one, sir,' she said.
> 'Then neither do I condemn you,' Jesus declared. 'Go now and leave your life of sin.'" (John 8:9-11)

Suddenly, this woman is alone in public with Jesus. She's guilty as sin. There's no defense. She was caught in the act, dragged in front of a bunch of judgmental men, where she becomes a pawn for their religious argument. She pulls the fabric of her skimpy top together so that at least she might die with some dignity, staring at the ground in hopeless shame.

And then everyone leaves. The sinners have all fled and she is left alone with Jesus, the one man who is without sin, the only one who could rightly condemn her. He is also the only man who saw her as a person and not as a pawn, maybe the only man who ever truly loved her for who she was instead of what she could do.

This awkward moment becomes her moment of salvation, where Jesus offers her two gifts that would forever change her life: forgiveness and encouragement.

The forgiveness is a big deal because he's the only one qualified to make such an offer. Jesus is the only one who could have thrown the stones of judgement, who could have executed the requirements of that ancient law that demanded her life.

But, instead, he offers grace. There is no condemnation in the presence of Jesus.

You and I are not qualified to judge other human beings. In fact, Jesus specifically warns us not to judge others (Matthew 7:1-2).

Instead we, like all sinners, need to drop our stones of unfair judgment and leave our fellow sinners in the hands of the only one who could condemn but instead forgives.

Abandon Your Life of Sin

Jesus doesn't just forgive her; he also encourages her to live her best life. When Jesus tells her, "leave your life of sin" he is declaring that she no longer needs to be defined by her seedy reputation, that she is no slave to sin, that who she is as a person is more than her past failures. Go, leave this life of sin.

"Freddy, I don't condemn you," Jesus would say to *Queen*'s lead singer. "But go, leave your life of sin."

What does that mean, exactly?

For the woman caught in adultery, it meant expressing her sexuality in a loving relationship and not in the hot pursuit of another lustful tryst. It meant honoring herself enough to pursue a relationship of genuine love where her sexuality might flourish in the shelter of a committed, loving marriage. The problem with adultery is that it oversteps the God-given bounds of relationships, it trespasses into an intimacy that exceeds commitment. Marriage is designed to fence in sexual intimacy to protect us in our most vulnerable state. Ironically, this fence of loving commitment leads to sexual freedom while sex without boundaries results in abuse and bondage.

Jesus wants the best for this woman, not a life where she doesn't know whose bed she'll wake up in tomorrow. He is inviting her to quit ignoring the God-given boundaries of relationships and to live with dignity and love. Jesus isn't telling her to never have sex again, but rather to do it right, to find freedom in commitment.

Jesus obviously knows that she will sin in the future. But she no longer needs to be defined by her sin and no longer needs to willingly surrender to it as a moral slave.

Freddy Mercury, like many gay men of his era, experimented sexually in ways that were unhealthy to his soul and body. Casual sex is lust-focused, not relationship-focused. By all accounts, there was a marked difference in Freddy Mercury's life when he finally found a love that led to commitment. Though unable to legally marry, Jim Hutton exchanged wedding bands with Freddy and they lived in a committed relationship for the last six years of Freddy Mercury's life.

To go and sin no more is to abandon a lust-driven life in exchange for a love-driven life. It is to see the value of your own life, that you are not merely a sinner, hopelessly enslaved to animal instincts and insatiable appetites. It is standing alone with Jesus, the one person who could rightfully condemn you, and accept his offer of total forgiveness and the necessary encouragement to go and sin no more. It is also seeing the value of others, that they are not underlings to be used for your own gratification, but fellow human beings, made in the image of God, inherently worthy of your love and respect.

If we interpret the phrase "Go and leave your life of sin" to mean "Quit being gay" then we stumble back into the kind of judgmental mindset that drags one type of sinner before Jesus while leaving the others offstage. We ignore the mounting evidence of science that indicates that sexual orientation is less a personal choice than a biological or hormonal state of being. Jesus doesn't tell the woman to quit being who she is, but rather to be that person in a way that honors herself, others, and the one who created her.

My Jesus, who loves gays, accepts them as they are.

Don't overlook the men leaving the scene of this potential stoning. When Jesus calls them out, "Let any one of you who is without sin be the first to throw a stone at her," the older men are first to recognize the hypocrisy of the moment. I understand that, because the older I get the less morally arrogant I've become. I see my own weakness and failure, and while I may sin in different ways than this woman, I am no less totally dependant on the grace of God offered to me in Jesus.

So I'm not throwing stones, not at those caught in adultery and not at those whose orientation or sexual identity differs from mine. I join those who humbly walk away from the arena of condemnation and let Jesus bestow his gift of forgiveness and his offer of new life.

Jesus didn't come into the world to condemn us, but to save us. And those who follow Jesus, who truly care about following the real, historic Jesus, are called to drop their stones of moral judgement, and instead offer encouragement to others, that they no longer need to be defined by the guilt and shame of their sin, but rather by the one who saves us all from our sin.

5

Go and Do Likewise

The ministry of Jesus was so focused on love that he was often quizzed about what it means to love others. The Parable of the Good Samaritan, which is recorded in Luke 10, was his response to one such question.

The occasion was an expert in the law testing Jesus by asking him, "Teacher, what must I do to inherit eternal life?" (Luke 10:25).

While this religious lawyer was testing Jesus, trying to make him look like an idiot or prove that he was a heretic, he does ask a good question. Every healthy human soul should ask during this lifetime what we must do to inherit eternal life.

Jesus is not one to be tricked, not even by a cunning lawyer. He is God in the flesh, after all, the most clever person to ever walk this earth. So he turns the question back on the lawyer:

> "What is written in the Law?" he replied. "How do you read it?"
>
> He answered: "'Love the Lord your God with all your heart and with all your soul and with all your strength and with all your mind'; and, 'Love your neighbor as yourself.'"
>
> "You have answered correctly," Jesus replied. "Do this and you will live." (Luke 10:26-28)

This is not quite the answer you would expect from an expert in the Jewish law. It appears that he has been tailing Jesus, taking notes on his teachings, and is now quoting Jesus back to Jesus.

Redefining the Law

The expected answer from an expert in the law would have been
what is called the *Shema*, which is the Hebrew word for "hear". The
Shema is a recital of Deuteronomy 6:4-9, which begins:

> "Hear *(shema)*, O Israel: The Lord our God, the Lord is
> one. Love the Lord your God with all your heart and
> with all your soul and with all your strength. These
> commandments that I give you today are to be upon
> your hearts. . . " (Deuteronomy 6:4-9)

Notice that the love for God is associated immediately with knowing
and keeping the commandments. It is a law-based relationship. The
expert in the law knew this by heart, in the original Hebrew, and yet
chose to quote Jesus' answer to the question instead.

Jesus, in his teaching, had altered the *Shema*, which was more
radical than someone altering our national anthem, pledge of allegiance,
or constitution. He did it because our relationship with God no longer
depends on laws, but on love.

Here's what Jesus did to the *Shema:*

> "One of them, an expert in the law, tested him with this
> question: "Teacher, which is the greatest commandment
> in the Law?"
>
> Jesus replied: "'Love the Lord your God with all
> your heart and with all your soul and with all your
> mind.' This is the first and greatest commandment. And
> the second is like it: 'Love your neighbor as yourself.'
> All the Law and the Prophets hang on these two
> commandments." (Matthew 22:35-40)

Jesus is actually combining verses from Deuteronomy 6 and Leviticus
19 into a new "law," the law of love. Scot McKnight calls this *the Jesus
Creed.* It is the core of Jesus' teaching, the heart of his own life, and the
guiding principle for all who follow Jesus. It replaces the law of the Old
Testament with its fulfillment: the law of love.

Before Jesus, the way a godly person showed love for God was by keeping the commandments in the Torah, what we call the Old Testament Law. Knowing and teaching the Torah was the bread and butter of this expert in the law who is testing Jesus in Luke 10. To be sure, there is a lot of love in that old law, but there's also a lot of law in that law, a lot of joyless restrictions and regulations that lure its followers into a mire of legalistic rule keeping.

What Jesus does, and what is at stake in this encounter with an expert in the law, is redefine how we love God. According to Jesus, we love God by loving others, by loving our neighbor. This is a huge change in how people approach God and how holiness is understood.

In Luke 10, this expert in the law doesn't give Jesus the traditional *Shema* answer, he gives Jesus the Jesus answer, the Jesus Creed. At least in theory he has accepted that God is more interested in love than in laws, and that the command to love our neighbors overpowers all other commands.

This expert, however, is not done with Jesus:

"But he wanted to justify himself, so he asked Jesus, 'And who is my neighbor?'" (Luke 10:29)

This was a question devout Jews spent time debating. They concluded that your neighbor was someone who was ritually clean, spiritually pure, and holy. According to the Torah, a person needed to separate themselves from an unclean world and devote themselves to all things holy, pure, and ceremonially clean. Thus a neighbor was a person who would aid in the quest to maintain ritual purity.

This was the life of this expert in the law. You love God by keeping rules, by staying clean, by avoiding anything in the world that might tarnish your reputation or stain your soul. As he questions Jesus, this man is trying to preserve his old religion, the comfort of his legalism. He is trying to justifying himself and guard his own pride. He is looking for the loophole, a way in which an expert in the law like himself, whose concern is the letter of the law more than the heart of the law, can still go home at the end of the day justified.

Unlike those bound to the law, Jesus had a very broad definition of who we are to love. In the Sermon on the Mount Jesus taught:

"You have heard that it was said, 'Love your neighbor and hate your enemy.' But I tell you: Love your enemies and pray for those who persecute you, that you may be children of your Father in heaven." (Matthew 5:43-45)

Expanding Our Neighborhood

The expert in the law must have missed that lecture. So Jesus tells him a story, answering his question with a parable:

"In reply Jesus said: 'A man was going down from Jerusalem to Jericho, when he fell into the hands of robbers. They stripped him of his clothes, beat him and went away, leaving him half dead.'" (Luke 10:30)

The crowd listening to Jesus tell this story was Jewish, as was Jesus. So it is assumed that this man on the road to Jericho was a Jewish man.

The road to Jericho was narrow, winding through steep valleys with rocky cliffs. There were plenty of places to hide in order to stage an ambush. It wasn't a busy route, so a bleeding person could easily die on the side of the road.

"A priest happened to be going down the same road, and when he saw the man, he passed by on the other side." (Luke 10:31)

This priest is a professional godly man. He served as a mediator between sinful people and a holy God. He should be an example of godliness.

And in this story he is! He is if you believe that a person shows their love for God by keeping the law to the letter. Here's what the law teaches:

"A priest must not make himself ceremonially unclean for any of his people who die, except for a close relative . . ." (Leviticus 21:1-2)

To be ceremonially unclean was to be ungodly, spiritually defiled in ways that would bar a person from entering God's holy presence. A priest could not fulfill his duties as dictated by the law when ceremonially unclean. And a priest:

> "will also be unclean if he touches something defiled by a corpse." (Leviticus 22:4)

In the days of Jesus, experts in the law had added to the law in an attempt to help people keep it more precisely. They taught that even the shadow of the priest should not touch a dead thing. This might explain why the priest went to the far side of the road to pass this beaten man, who was, most likely, already dead.

I'd always heard that the reason the priest didn't stop was that he was in a hurry, because he was such an important man. Perhaps that accounts for some of his indifference, but the real explanation is his desire to not be defiled, to remain holy and pleasing to God by keeping the letter of the law as spelled out in Leviticus.

The parable continues:

> "So too, a Levite, when he came to the place and saw him, passed by on the other side." (Luke 10:32)

Levites were godly people whose job it was to help the priests with their duties. They weren't the professional clergy so much as outstanding, regular Israelites. He too should be an example of godliness.

And in this story he is, at least if you think godliness comes from keeping the letter of the law. The Old Testament book of Numbers 19:11-12 says that any person, not just priests, who "touches the dead body of anyone will be unclean for seven days. He must purify himself with the water on the third day . . ."

So naturally, in his attempt to please God, he sees the beaten man and, fearing he might be dead and unclean, goes around him and hurries off. He doesn't want to show up in Jericho unclean and thus unfit for duty, and he doesn't want to make all his family and friends unclean through contact with him.

Here's what Scot McKnight writes in his book, *The Jesus Creed*:

> There is not a Jew who hears Jesus' parable who thinks
> the priest (or the Levite) is doing anything but what the
> Torah regulates. The irony of his little plot is that in
> 'obeying' the Torah the priest and Levite are disobeying
> what is at the bottom of the Torah: loving others.[1]

Those listening to this parable were agreeing with Jesus so far,
nodding their heads. This is exactly what they expected, and exactly
what the expert in the law would have done had he been a character in
this story.

And then Jesus springs his own trap in order to teach the truth
about loving God by loving others:

> "But a Samaritan, as he traveled, came where the man
> was; and when he saw him, he took pity on him." (Luke
> 10:33)

The plot twist here is that the Samaritans were the enemies of Jewish
people. There was no love lost between Jews and Samaritans. Because
they differed religiously and ethnically, there was a long bitter history of
distrust and hatred.

So it is surprising that a Samaritan would have pity on a beaten
Jew. It seems more likely he would smile and finished him off. But his
actions defy such expectations:

> "He went to him and bandaged his wounds, pouring on
> oil and wine. Then he put the man on his own donkey,
> took him to an inn and took care of him. The next day
> he took out two silver coins and gave them to the
> innkeeper. 'Look after him,' he said, 'and when I return,
> I will reimburse you for any extra expense you may
> have.'" (Luke 10:34-35)

Despite centuries of racial hatred between the two peoples, at
great expense and inconvenience to himself, risking his own personal
safety on this desolate road, this stranger helps another human being.

He is the original Good Samaritan.

Jesus' point here is that the Samaritan loved this man, that he showed his love for God by loving another person, even if that person is not only a stranger, but an enemy whose values and way of life contradicts his own.

Now Jesus asks the final question to complete his lesson:

"Which of these three do you think was a neighbor to the man who fell into the hands of robbers?" (Luke 10:36)

Instead of trying to limit love, as the expert in the law was trying to do by defining "neighbor" as narrowly as possible, Jesus is trying to stretch the boundaries of love. His love includes all: not just those who look like us, or share our ethnicity, or hold to the same religion, or those who can reciprocate our acts of love and kindness.

The shock in this story is the identity of the person who turns out to be the good neighbor. The expert in the law cannot even utter the word "Samaritan":

"The expert in the law replied, 'The one who had mercy on him.' Jesus told him, 'Go and do likewise.'" (Luke 10:37)

Clever Jesus gets the self-righteous, self-important lawyer to answer his own question, but in a way in which he never wanted it answered.

The expert in the law knows that we are to love God and love our neighbor, but he is trying to limit his love by defining "neighbor" in a way that excludes most people. Jesus uses this simple story to stretch the idea of neighbor to include people living in a tent city, people who enter our country illegally, people who voted for the wrong candidate, people whose values and lifestyle do not correspond to ours.

Everyone.

Jesus is trying here, and everywhere, to expand love, to extend the boundaries of our love.

This parable did that for those who first heard it.

We miss some of the impact of this parable because the word "Samaritan" has evolved into something good, but it wasn't to those who first listened to Jesus' story. A Samaritan was vile, a person not to be trusted, a person who would never help someone like you, and so you should never help someone like them.

But Jesus is teaching that we love God by loving others, even enemies.

A Higher Law

Jesus teaches us something else about love in this parable that I've overlooked in the past: What happens when loving someone is in conflict with the Old Testament law?

Here's how Scot McKnight frames the question:

> What happens when love-of-God-as-obeying-Torah (the *Shema* of Judaism) comes into conflict with love-of-God-as-following-Jesus (the *Shema* of Jesus)? That's a tough one, for all of us. But for Jesus the answer is clear: Loving God properly always means that we will tend to those in need.[2]

The Samaritan violated the laws in Leviticus, made himself "unclean" in order to show love to the man beaten on the side of the road. But just as when Jesus touched the leper, the Samaritan's loving kindness brings holiness to the scene, not the expected spread of ritual uncleanliness to him.

Jesus isn't just telling stories. He lived this no-boundaries love. When he touch the leper to show love he was clearly violating the letter of the old law. The woman with a medical condition of bleeding didn't contaminate Jesus with her touch, but instead was healed by her faith in him (Matthew 9:20-22). Jesus' actions and words all clearly teach that the law of love overrides, overpowers, and overshadows the antiquated law of rules.

Sadly, in our culture, some people who claim to follow Jesus have aligned themselves with the priest and Levite. They spout out verses from Leviticus as if that alone summarizes the essence of their faith. They declare that LGBTQ people are an abomination, hated by God and condemned to hell. They are merely adding to the world's prejudice and hatred.

True followers of Jesus will, instead, heed his teaching and stop to help those beaten almost to death by the world's disdain for LGBTQ people. At great cost to themselves and their reputation, they imitate this good Samaritan and tend to those in need of our love and care.

Jesus doesn't negate the law or destroy the law. He fulfills the law. Love for neighbor is indeed in the book of Leviticus, but tucked away where it was overshadowed by all these other rules. Jesus brings to the forefront the law of love—that we love God, we love Jesus, by loving others.

The "new command" of Jesus to love one another (John 13:34-35) is technically not new at all. But elevating love as the defining way in which we show our holiness and our devotion to God is new with Jesus. To allow love to define all other laws and to free us from misusing the laws in ways that made the priest and the Levite act with loveless indifference, is refreshingly new.

It isn't lawlessness—it is the perfect law of love.

The Perfect Law

There is no teaching, no law, no commandments that override the law of love. The love Jesus teaches is spelled out in the rest of the New Testament, in places like Galatians 5:

> "But the fruit of the Spirit is love, joy, peace, patience, kindness, goodness, faithfulness, gentleness and self-control. Against such things there is no law."
> (Galatians 5:22-23)

Everything else flows from love. There is no law higher than the law of love, which produces all of these other fruits.

Against love there is no law.

If we always love like Jesus loves, then there is no need for any other rules. Scripture, and even many of the laws in it, can help us figure out how to best love others, but if we always act in a loving way toward others, we are not bound by any other laws or commandments.

The challenge that Jesus lays out for the expert in the law is the same challenge for anyone who takes Jesus seriously: "Do likewise."

Love is something we do. Love is action, not mere sentiment, not religious feelings. Love is treating everyone like a neighbor, actively meeting their needs.

It is how we show our love for God, according to Jesus. Not by memorizing the many laws of the book of Leviticus and making sure we and everyone else keep them all, but doing something that is much more difficult: loving one another.

Jesus himself is our model for this love. Jesus found us all left for dead on the side of the road, beat up by sin, dying in shame, lost in guilt, utterly helpless. He didn't step around us on our road to Jericho. He gave himself for us; his love was proved by his actions. He gave far more than the use of his donkey and some silver coins: Jesus gave his own life for us on the cross.

That has become the definition of love:

> "This is love: not that we loved God, but that he loved us and sent his Son as an atoning sacrifice for our sins. Dear friends, since God so loved us, we also ought to love one another." (1 John 4:10-11)

High Cost, High Reward

We have cheapened the term Good Samaritan when we think it refers only to helping a stranded motorist or paying for someone's groceries. In this parable Jesus is calling us to a selfless, sacrificial love in a world that desperately needs genuine expressions of that love. To the extent that we follow Jesus, we must offer the compassion and love of Jesus to those who identify as LGBTQ.

This love is not just tolerance. Rather it is genuine care, tangible kindness shown in helpful actions. Scot McKnight writes:

> Because our society has elevated tolerance to the highest of virtues, our society remains confused about what love means. Christians are not called to tolerance; Christians are called to love. Toleration condescends; love honors.[3]

I've taken it as a personal challenge to do my best to honor LGBTQ people as image-bearers of God, beloved by God. Too many pastors and church leaders have treated them like the Jews treated the Samaritans. Good Christian people stay far enough away from gay people so that not even their shadows mingle. The result is that LGBTQ people believe that all Christians hate them and our churches will not welcome them.

That's not right, not if we follow Jesus.

My Jesus loves gays. He calls us to do the same.

I preached this parable in my church a few years ago and used it to challenge our church to greater compassion toward LGBTQ people. That was the last time one particular family ever attended our church. They accused me of selling out the truth and being too kind to gay people. I learned that if a pastor in a conservative church wants to remain "clean" he oughtn't even approach the shadow of this subject.

Meanwhile the Samaritan, the one Jesus holds up as our example, has the blood of the beaten on his clothes. I wonder if the Good Samaritan's brothers considered him a traitor for helping this good-for-nothing Jew. Was his wife upset that he squandered two silver coins on a stranger? Was he considered a sell-out because he aligned himself with someone whose values contradict his own?

Choosing love may not help our reputation, but it is the way of Jesus. The Good Samaritan was poorer financially and his reputation was tarnished, but he was richer spiritually and more blessed because of his Christlike love.

Go, Be the Neighbor

When Jesus tells this expert in the law: "Go and do likewise," he was not just sending the man away, dismissing him now that he had answered his trick questions. Jesus was challenging him, along with us all, to not ignore the needs of the world around us, to not step to the far side of the road in order to avoid contact with the messy problems of life. It's too easy to look away, to ignore needs so that we don't have to respond with Good Samaritan love.

The challenge "to go" is to venture down the Jericho roads and look for ways to show love and kindness to those injured and overlooked.

It is easy to simply overlook the needs of the LGBTQ community if you aren't gay. It is easy to step to the other side of the road, claiming that such actions will keep the church unblemished and holy, that shunning our gay children will maintain the honor of our family.

But that isn't what Jesus does and it isn't what he wants us to do. The way of the Good Samaritan, the way of Jesus, is engaging those who need our love, even if such contact might violate some lesser law, even if others consider us defiled because of our compassion, even if it costs us our good reputation. It is seeing the person in need not as Jewish or Samaritan, straight or gay, but as neighbor.

The LGBTQ people I know, especially teens and young adults, are beaten up by the world's hatred and prejudice. How can we not be neighbors to them?

If we are faithful to Jesus, we need to allow the law of love to overshadow the laws of Leviticus and allow the Holy Spirit to lead us in meaningful ministry to that community. We need to get off our donkey and tend to the needs of the beaten and forgotten.

6

Love is Love

Love is the defining characteristic of a life well lived, according to Jesus. Love is the litmus test for the quality of actions and the moral choices made by those who follow Jesus. Every act of selfless love makes the world more the way God intended it to be. Love is, in short, the moral logic behind everything Jesus taught and everything he did.

Moral logic is the ethical foundation, the deep truth that supports particular teachings or actions. Moral logic probes the reason behind the commandments. It explains actions. It answers the question of motivation.

For example, the Bible teaches:

> "Does not the very nature of things teach you that if a man has long hair, it is a disgrace to him, but that if a woman has long hair, it is her glory?" (1 Corinthians 11:14-15)

What's funny is that most of the pictures we see of Jesus have him with long hair, which was apparently disgraceful in Corinth but not in Galilee, where Jesus lived. When we ask why long hair on men was disgraceful we are trying to uncover the moral logic beneath this text. Most of us personally know long-haired men and short-haired women who are not a disgrace, who are beautiful and kind. So we know that there is something behind this verse, some deeper moral logic that needs to be identified so that we understand what is really at issue in this statement.

33

Without moral logic, (that is, if we simply took every command and every teaching in every Bible verse literally, without deeper thought or interpretation) Bible-believing Christians would always greet each other with a kiss instead of the current practice of a handshake or hug. We would refrain from wearing any clothes that have any mixture of fabrics. We wouldn't eat most seafood. Christians would almost never divorce and, if they did, they would almost never remarry. Women would not be allowed to speak in church at all. And we would still be justified in owning other human beings as slaves.

Clearly we apply a moral logic to our interpretation of the Bible. No one just reads the Bible, takes it literally, and then lives what it teaches. That would actually be a violation of the moral logic of the very Bible that this person would be trying to honor.

Since Jesus is the main character of the Bible, a biblical moral logic that will consistently interpret the rest of scripture must come from Jesus. For Jesus, sacrificial love is the moral logic that defines all of his teaching, determines his every action, and guides his understanding of scripture.

Love Guides

When we aren't clear about a certain decision, when the right or wrong position on a complicated issue is puzzling, when we aren't sure how to respond to a particular person, love always turns out to be the right answer, every single time. If we simply follow the example of Christlike love then we have made the right choice. This is why the Bible says, "Against such things there is no law." (Galatians 5:23). For those who follow Jesus, "The only thing that counts is faith expressing itself through love." (Galatians 5:6). Such love is not a free-for-all, but it does free us to choose a course of action consistent with God's unconditional love.

My daughter, Natalie, asked if I would perform her wedding. She had met Rachel in college and, after several years of dating, they decided to get married. I had done some reading and thinking about gay marriage, but at that time wasn't completely sure that it was supported by the Bible. What I did know, beyond a doubt, is that I loved both Natalie and Rachel, and that not being a part of their wedding would hang a cloud of regret over our future relationship. It was love that drove me to officiate their wedding more than my understanding of the biblical texts surrounding homosexuality.

In explaining my decision to other pastors I have quoted 1 Peter 4:8, "Above all, love each other deeply, because love covers over a multitude of sins." I don't believe that the girls getting married was a sin nor do I believe that my officiating the wedding was sinful. What is clear is that when our motives are the deep love of Jesus it hardly matters. Love covers an array of mistakes and a multitude of sins.

If we are to understand the Bible's teaching on any subject, especially gender, sexuality, and marriage, we have to read each passage in light of the moral logic of Jesus' love. God's desire for every human being is that we live in love, that his love is made complete by our love for others.

Lust is Anti-Love

The opposite of love is lust. Lust is desire gone haywire, desire for the wrong things or fulfilling desire through the wrong means. Lust is misdirected and unrestrained desire that ignores and destroys the bounds of decency, kindness, and order. While love focuses on others, lust is self-obsessed.

Lust isn't just a sexual term. Lust for power leads to abusive relationship and corrupt governing. Hatred is a deadly form of lust that desires harm for others. Lust for money and material goods leads to theft and social injustice. And sexual lust leads to abuse and the destruction of healthy relationships. Lust is inherently self-seeking, almost always at the expense of others. It focuses on self-gratification, stealing power and dignity from others to gets its own way. Lust uses people for its own will and pleasure. The Bible defines lust as actions that "indulge the sinful nature." (Galatians 5:13). Such lust is mirror opposite to sacrificial love.

All of the scriptures in the Bible that teach against homosexual activity do so in the context of lust, not love. There's only a handful of Bible passages that explicitly address homosexual behavior, which I'll address more carefully in Chapter 9. Without exception, all of these verses condemn lust, not love. The same lust is also condemned in heterosexual activity because it uses people, abuses others, and is anti-God because it is anti-love.

It is lust that swirls about in our hearts and minds whenever we sin. Sin arises from lustful wanting, unbridled desire, and a focus so intensely selfish that it is blinded to its effects on others and to any sense of right and wrong. Whether it is lust for power, for things, or for pleasure, it compels us to indulge ourselves at the expense of others.

Lust can be desiring what is evil and destructive, but it can also be desiring good things in bad ways, without the boundaries of decency and self-control. While some consider all homosexuality a lusty distortion of healthy sexuality, others see the genuine love that exists in gay relationships just as clearly as it does in straight couples.

Because all of the Bible's teachings about homosexual activities focus on lust, they simply do not directly address the issue of a healthy gay relationship. James V. Brownson writes:

> We define the words "gay" and "lesbian," not first of all
> by behavior, but by sexual orientation; this is not at all
> the same thing as lust, which is understood as excessive
> desire.[1]

Ancient civilization had no concept of sexual orientation and therefore did not imagine a loving, gay relationship. The Bible's condemnation of lustful, selfish, and abusive homosexuality is as true and relevant as its condemnation of heterosexual sin, but does not apply to the kind of loving, mutually beneficial relationship that so many gay couples enjoy today.

More Than Nice Ideas and Good Intentions

I am a pastor in a denomination that, unfortunately, has not considered how the moral logic of love informs our interpretation of scripture, and therefore does not allow its clergy to perform gay weddings. Officiating Natalie and Rachel's wedding was not meant to be an act of defiance against my church, but rather an act of love. I believe I was following the moral logic of love instead of the antiquated rules of a traditional denomination.

Despite the wedding being a private event with very few guests, word has gotten out through some malicious gossip that I performed a gay wedding. (Gossip can still be gossip even if it is true, and this happens to be true gossip). A few of my more conservative pastoral colleagues are up in arms and want me to be disciplined by the church, perhaps a suspension without pay or a complete end to my career.

One pastor, who just won't leave me alone, asked if the church should also allow a pastor who is a white supremacist to continue teaching racist ideas. Should we also turn a blind eye to evidence of a sexually abusive pastor, he asked me. He believes, like many traditional Christians, that the only way to support gay marriage is to abandon the authority of the Bible in favor of a watered-down religion of nice ideas and good intentions.

While it is true that some churches have wandered from biblical authority in their attempt to be more open and affirming toward LGBTQ persons, the real solution is to focus more intensely on Jesus, to imitate the radical love he offered to everyone he encountered, and to allow such love to transform the way our churches minister to the LGBTQ community. Instead of distancing ourselves from the Bible, this is a call to cling more tightly to the Bible's central character.

It seems as if this pastor has never considered the moral logic of love. White supremacy is born of lustful hate, a self-centered world view that steals power by degrading others based on racial differences. And sexual abuse is the ultimate in uncontrolled lust.

When Jesus fulfilled the law and the prophets, he replaced the legalistic code with the single command to love one another. When we wonder whether a particular law from the Old Testament continues to be a guiding principle for our lives we need only ask whether it meets the criteria of love.

This love is not merely nice ideas and good intentions. Jesus demonstrated his love by selflessly meeting the needs of those around him, by kneeling down to wash the dirty feet of his own disciples, by surrendering his life to the torturous death on a cross. This is not a cutesy, feel-good emotion; it is real love.

To compare lust-based behavior like racism and sexual abuse to performing the wedding of two committed, loving people is to completely miss the point of Jesus' moral logic. While this pastor believes his position to be biblically superior to mine because he has taken the historically traditional view, he is completely mistaken. His stance against gay marriage and his actions against me are judgmental, hurtful, and ultimately hateful.

I've come to quite the opposite conclusion based on the moral logic of Christ's love. Jesus sought out the dispossessed, the down and out, the lepers who were rejected by society, family, and religion. And he loved them. He embraced them publicly. He validated them as real people, no less children of God than anyone else.

The teaching on marriage in both the Old and New Testaments is focused on loving commitment, sacrificial service, and mutual submission, not the gender of the participants. Many have mistakenly confused cultural traditions and historic norms for biblical teaching while overlooking the Bible's unmistakable teaching on love and acceptance.

My conclusion is that Christians should be the loudest supporters of gay rights and gay marriage. We should stand up for the dignity of our fellow human beings, even if they are sexually oriented or identify sexually in a way that differs from us. Such differences disappear in importance when we offer the genuine love that Christ so freely offers to us.

7

Open Table, New Wine

Calling Christians to stand up for gay rights as basic human rights, for churches to truly welcome LGBTQ people, and for pastors to perform gay weddings is, in most cases, a call to radical change, a quantum shift in understanding and actions.

One barrier to Christians becoming more welcoming and inviting is that churches naturally resist change because they are defined by the ancient and unchangeable text of the Bible. The church doesn't form its policies by opinion polls or through popular vote. Christian churches wrestle with their sacred Scripture, and even then resist change based on a fear of selling out to culture, never wanting to become too worldly.

Jesus had to deal with this stubborn resistance to change. The fifth chapter of Luke's gospel records a series of unconventional actions and teachings by Jesus, which include the touching of a leper in order to heal him, forgiving the sins of a man paralyzed from birth and then healing him in order to prove he had the authority to forgive sins, calling a tax collector as a disciple, and finally eating at his house with the kind of scoundrels and lowlifes that normally dine with tax collectors. The chapter ends with Jesus being questioned about all this newness by the guardians of the old religion.

The Pharisees and the teachers of the law specifically questioned Jesus about his dinner guests: "Why do you eat and drink with tax collectors and 'sinners'?" (Luke 5:30).

They complained because who you ate with spoke volumes about your character. Your dining guests revealed your values and morals. The religious old order was questioning Jesus' character because

39

he was eating at a tax collector's home in the company of known sinners.

If he followed the Old Testament teachings on cleanliness, Jesus never would have eaten with tax collectors, sinners, or even Gentiles. It's all spelled out in the book of Leviticus, which teaches that you are unclean if you serve the wrong kind of food, if you have certain diseases, if it is your time of the month, if you are wearing the wrong clothes, even if you have touched anything unclean. Clean people don't eat with unclean people because that would make them unclean. In fact, anything unclean: food, clothes, or a person, would make the table unclean and the people eating at that table equally unclean.

There were, of course, rituals one could go through to become clean again, at least in most cases. They involved washing a particular way, waiting a certain amount of time, and making very detailed sacrifices. It was all regulated by Levitical law. It was a rigorous ritual to go from unclean to clean, so you certainly did not want people at your table whose very presence would make you unclean.

Who you dined with was a religious statement. Devout God-fearing people would not tolerate unclean people at their table. No one labeled a "sinner" or ceremonially unclean was welcome at their table or, for that matter, even in their home. You showed your piety, your devotion to God and his law, by only eating ceremonially clean food with equally clean people.

Room for All

Jesus turned the tables on who is welcome at his table. Up to this moment, especially in the religious world of the times, a person had to purify themselves and then, when ritually clean, they could come to the table. Jesus turned this upside down by saying that anyone is welcome at his table, just as they are, sinners and tax collectors alike, and that their presence at the table of Christ is the very thing that makes them pure. The act of eating and spending time with Jesus begins the relationship that makes them clean.

Instead of requiring purity, Jesus creates it. He offers rest to the spiritually weary, an easy yoke to the already heavily burdened. Jesus' table is a place of grace where he humbles himself to eat with any who will pull up a chair.

By welcoming all people: tax collectors, public sinners, even the teachers of the law and the Pharisees, Jesus is showing that his table creates a new society, one that finds its unity in his love and acceptance. That society expands when its members love and accept others with that same gracious hospitality.

Part of that new society is equality. Peter the fisherman is no better than Matthew the tax collector, the prostitute no worse than the Pharisee. We are all equally unworthy of being at this table with Jesus. There is not a person at the table of Jesus who belongs there except that Jesus himself invites us. None of us are worthy.

So we cannot look down our noses at people who might seem less holy than we are. We can't say, "You're unclean. Clean up your act and then come back and we'll see if there is room for you." That is not the table of Jesus.

Looking through the window of Matthew's house, with tax collectors and sinners gathered around Jesus, one cannot conclude that LGBTQ people are worse sinners than others. The picture is quite the opposite. No one is worthy and yet everyone is invited to the table of Jesus.

One of my favorite doughnut shops has a sign in the window which reads: "We welcome all races and ethnicities, all religions, all countries of origin, all gender identities, all sexual orientations, all abilities and disabilities, all spoken languages, all ages, everyone." Isn't that what a church centered on Jesus should have on their front door?

This is not the way that the Pharisees and teachers of the law viewed religion. They demanded an explanation of why Jesus would dine with such a motley crew of sinners.

The New Wine

In response Jesus tells them a short parable, really more of an object lesson:

> "No one tears a patch from a new garment and sews it on an old one. If he does, he will have torn the new garment, and the patch from the new will not match the old. And no one pours new wine into old wineskins. If

he does, the new wine will burst the skins, the wine will run out and the wineskins will be ruined. No, new wine must be poured into new wineskins. And no one after drinking old wine wants the new, for he says, 'The old is better.'" (Luke 5:36-39)

In those days it was common to drink wine with your meal. Wine was often stored in skins, which allowed for the expansion of the wine as it fermented and matured. Everyone knew you didn't store new wine in old wine skins because the old skins would have dried out and become brittle. They could not expand. Using old wine skins would always end in disaster, the skin was ruined and the wine wasted.

What God was doing through the ministry of Jesus was so new that it was like new wine requiring new skins. The Pharisees taught a religion of rules, full of fasting, excessive praying, and trying to measure up to God's perfect standards.

In contrast, Jesus came and welcomed foul-mouthed fishermen as disciples, offered forgiveness to the discarded, and called a corrupt tax-collector to follow him.

There is something new and radical about Jesus' ministry.

There was something dated and stale in the religion of the Pharisees. Their old wine had soured to vinegar. Jesus comes along and offers the sweet taste of mercy and the satisfying cup of love that was always lacking in their rule-based religion.

The new wine is Jesus. It is his love and forgiveness.

The New Covenant

Christian churches celebrate communion (which some call the Eucharist or the Lord's Supper). It commemorates the last supper that Jesus had with his disciples before his crucifixion. He used this occasion to prepare them for what was about to happen, to reshape their relationship with God through the events they were about to witness.

Part of the old religion, the old covenant, was the Passover. It dates back to the Exodus and celebrates the salvation of God's people. Jesus redefines the Passover as pointing to himself:

"In the same way, after the supper he took the cup, saying, 'This cup is the new covenant in my blood, which is poured out for you.' (Luke 22:20)

Jesus is completely redefining the Jewish religion, instituting a new covenant in his own blood. He is the Lamb of God who takes away the sins of the world.

Matthew's account of this same moment gets to the heart of that covenant:

"Then he took the cup, and when he had given thanks, he gave it to them, saying, 'Drink from it, all of you. This is my blood of the covenant, which is poured out for many for the forgiveness of sins.'" (Matthew 26:27-28)

This is a covenant of grace not works, love not law. It is a covenant that offers forgiveness through the sacrifice of Jesus and, unlike the old covenant, it is offered to all.

People who grew up in a Christian church, or even just in American culture with its many churches and Christian influence, miss just how new and revolutionary Jesus' teaching was. Those who idealize that old-time religion overlook the newness of Jesus' wine. He changed the way that we understand religion and the way in which we relate to God.

That reality, as much as anything else, is why Jesus was executed on a Roman cross. The old guard resisted change and decided that to kill the messenger might just kill the message.

That old wine of legalism, of judging people as clean or unclean, can pollute the cellars of our thinking and leave a bitter taste to our religion.

The new wine of forgiveness is so much better. When Jesus explains that it is the sick who need a doctor he is inviting us all to his table. By welcoming us Jesus heals our very souls. By accepting us he makes us acceptable to God. This allowed the cheating tax collector named Matthew to be called a disciple of Jesus, and for him to throw a holy party where he introduced the kind of people who had given up on religion to a new religion that focused entirely on Jesus. The new wine of this new covenant celebrates that at his table there is an open chair just for you.

Today's New Wine

We live in a unique period of history, a time when LGBTQ people can finally emerge from the shadows of public shame. In this new era, clinging to historical tradition as if it were binding scripture is like drinking rancid vinegar while pretending it's wine. Allowing the all-accepting love of Jesus and the newness of his gospel message to guide us in welcoming our gay brothers and sisters into the church, into our lives, is the fresh wine of the new covenant.

The new wine of Jesus wasn't just for the first century; it continues to be poured out today. God is doing something new in Christ and his followers today. Part of that new wine is the inclusion of those who identify in non-traditional categories of gender, those whose sexual preferences don't conform to traditional norms. These are exactly the kind of people, overlooked by society, rejected by family, who Jesus welcomes, whose company he seems to enjoy, to whom he offers the new wine of his life-changing mercy.

A mistaken part of being a conservative Christian is the belief that our faith never changes, that truth doesn't adapt to culture. That is just the sour grapes of Pharisees who oppose the living wine of Jesus.

Richard Hays has written against the church accepting LGBTQ people. Part of his appeal is to historical tradition:

> Far more emphatically than scripture itself, the moral teaching tradition of the Christian church has for more than nineteen hundred years declared homosexual behavior to be contrary to the will of God.[1]

Jesus' parable of the new wine and new wineskins makes it impossible to simply appeal to history to settle the argument about accepting LGBTQ people. The fact that the church has traditionally shunned homosexuals is not a valid argument for continuing injustice and bigotry today. Stale faith grounded in history and tradition is not the dynamic faith of those following Jesus. If we try to stifle the wine and contain it in dried-out skins, it will only burst our faith.

While it is challenging to examine your own faith, hold it up to the light of Christ's new work in you, the living wine of his love. See if he isn't calling you to expand the reaches of your love, to extend the same grace and mercy that God, in Christ, extends to you.

The truth is that Bible-believing Christians do change their beliefs in light of cultural changes. Slavery was normal in Bible times and accepted by the Christian church for many centuries. The New Testament teaching that addressed both slaves and slave owners may have tempered slavery, but the writers of biblical texts did not imagine a time when human slavery would cease to exist. While Bible passages were once twisted to condone ongoing slavery, all Christians now understand that the moral logic of love and the teachings on universal human dignity do imagine a time when slavery is nothing more than a sad footnote in history.

The Christian church's teaching on divorce has also adapted due to the legalization of divorce and the prevalence of divorce in America. As opposed to homosexuality, Jesus actually had a lot to say about divorce. His words have not changed, but the church has seasoned them with the salt of mercy and a generous portion of grace.

Pharisee logic clings to the past and defines relationship through rules, especially our relationship with God. Jesus' new wine is the mercy of his love, a love which cannot be contained by the old skins of antiquated, misunderstood, and misapplied rules. This new wine skin is always expanding to offer his love to more and more people.

Those who fix their eyes on Jesus instead of mere religion will welcome LGBTQ people to the table of mercy where the wine of acceptance flows to tax collectors, sinners, and everyone else who accepts the offer and pulls up a chair.

8

The Light Yoke

It wasn't just the old religious guard who struggled with the new wine of Jesus' inclusive message of love and mercy; the early Christian church did too. They specifically wondered how the gospel applied to Gentiles, to those who were not part of their religious past, those who had historically been considered unclean. Did they have to clean up their act and adopt the laws of the old covenant in order to be allowed to approach the table of Jesus?

These questions arose when Paul, Barnabas, and others began evangelizing Gentiles. This may seem like a trivial ethnic distinction to us today, but to Jews and Jewish Christians this was the dividing label for all of humanity. Richard B. Hays writes:

> To be Gentile was, in the eyes of Jews and Jewish Christians alike, the same as being a sinner, since the Gentiles did not have the law, since they were by definition unclean, polluted, and idolatrous.[1]

Some of the Jewish Christians from Judea believed that Paul and Barnabas were, by preaching grace to the Gentiles in Antioch, cheapening the gospel. So they traveled to Antioch and demanded that the new converts be circumcised according to the laws of Moses as a condition for salvation (Acts 15:1).

Paul and Barnabas dug in their heels on their offer of grace. They debated the Jewish Christians from Judea and realized that it was too big of an issue to resolve locally in Antioch. A council of church leaders soon met in Jerusalem to discern how best to assimilate these new, Gentile believers into the church. The decisions of this council would define the future of the church as it expanded into the Gentile world.

Everyone was overjoyed that Gentiles had accepted Jesus as Christ, that the Messiah was no longer contained to the Jews but was savior of all nations. But some Christians who had once belonged to the party of the Pharisees demanded that the Gentiles must be circumcised and obey the law of Moses in order to be true Christians.

They were insisting that the new wine be stored in old wineskins.

Peter, who was a leader in the early church and was present when Jesus taught about new wine needing new wineskins, finally spoke up in defense of the Gentiles:

> "God, who knows the heart, showed that he accepted
> them by giving the Holy Spirit to them, just as he did to
> us. He did not discriminate between us and them, for he
> purified their hearts by faith. Now then, why do you try
> to test God by putting on the necks of Gentiles a yoke
> that neither we nor our ancestors have been able to
> bear? No! We believe it is through the grace of our Lord
> Jesus that we are saved, just as they are." (Acts 15:8-11)

The heavy yoke of the old law was more than anyone could bear, even lifelong devout Jews. So why burden these new and excited believers with unnecessary rules? Instead, Peter calls the church to celebrate the new wine of Jesus' love flowing beyond the Jewish race into all parts of the world.

James had the final word on the matter and set the tone for restored unity in the early church:

> "It is my judgment, therefore, that we should not make
> it difficult for the Gentiles who are turning to God.
> Instead we should write to them, telling them to abstain
> from food polluted by idols, from sexual immorality,
> from the meat of strangled animals and from blood. For
> the law of Moses has been preached in every city from
> the earliest times and is read in the synagogues on every
> Sabbath." (Acts 15:19-21)

James is applying the teaching of Jesus to the modern dilemma of his day. For those wishing to follow Jesus, the yoke is always easy and the burden must be kept light. James states a truth that should guide the church into the future, namely that we should never make it difficult for those who are turning to God. Adding rules from the old law will do nothing to add to the grace of Jesus Christ by which all are saved. In fact Paul teaches, in Galatians 5:2-4, that adding law to grace destroys grace altogether.

Circumcision was among the most important religious rites in Judaism, instituted in the days of Abraham, many centuries before Moses and the rest of the law. This was not a minor element of religious practice. This was the sign of the covenant between God and his chosen people, a normative practice that pre-dated the Jewish faith. It was a big deal.

And yet Paul writes these words dipped in new wine:

"For in Christ Jesus neither circumcision nor uncircumcision has any value. The only thing that counts is faith expressing itself through love." (Galatians 5:6)

The new wine of Christ requires only the wineskin of faith in Jesus which naturally produces love. In the end, this is the only thing that matters.

What the council in Jerusalem decided was that faith in Jesus, evidenced by genuine love, is the heart of the new covenant, not ancient rules and obsolete laws. Gentiles did not have to quit being practicing Gentiles by keeping the laws of Judaism in order to then be worthy of Christ. This was a seismic shift of inclusion that redefined who was a part of the Christian church.

No one, Jew or Gentile, gay or straight, is worthy of Christ. Yet all are invited to follow him in a life of faith and love.

There is a parallel between Gentile inclusion and the inclusion of LGBTQ persons in the life of the church. Both groups have been historically excluded based on their birth-identity. Both have been the victims of scripture passages used like poisonous darts. Both are loved by Jesus and welcomed into his kingdom.

Jeffrey Siker sees this as the best analogy for the modern church accepting gay Christians:

> Peter and Paul called the Jewish Christian church in their day to move beyond the marginal toleration of Gentile Christians to welcome their full inclusion. Similarly, in our day we in the heterosexual Christian church are being called by God to move beyond our marginal toleration of homosexual Christians to welcome their full inclusion.[2]

Though being Gentile was considered the equivalent of a godless sinner, Gentiles did not quit being Gentiles when they decided to follow Jesus. They were not healed of their Gentileness. They did not have to first become Jewish through a process of law-keeping and denouncing their Gentile ways, and then accept Jesus once fully divested of their Gentile identity. They just followed Jesus.

Those who believe that any LGBTQ person must first renounce their identity, conform to normative heterosexual desires, adopt Old Testament laws regulating sexuality, and then finally be worthy of accepting Jesus and entering the church, are ignoring this pivotal moment in the book of Acts. While there were several conditions placed on the Gentile believers in Antioch (which included refraining from sexual immorality), they continued to be uncircumcised Gentiles who belong to the church because they belong to Christ.

If Jesus welcomes people to himself and says that his burden is light, why would churches heap on the extra burden of a special set of rules for gay believers? Why would we stand between people, including LGBTQ people, and the God who loves them?

I want to pastor a church where LGBTQ people feel as comfortable in the presence of God as straight people, where together we walk humbly with Jesus. The church that adapted to include Gentiles can also adapt to welcome a group of people who may be different in certain ways, but are essentially the same as those already within the church community.

Keeping the Peace

There were a few concessions in Acts 15 regarding meat sacrificed to idols, sexual immorality, the meat of strangled animals, and blood. While that might seem like a random list, it was meant to guard the unity of the early church. It was carefully designed to help these new, Gentile Christians live among their Jewish brothers and sisters without insulting their Jewish consciences. It was about keeping peace in the early church, not keeping the law of the ancient faith.

The unity of the diverse church is always worth guarding. All of us should make allowances for the weaknesses and the hangups of others whose consciences are offended by our freedoms in Christ (Romans 14:15). Paul, who vehemently defended the fact that Christians need not be circumcised, nevertheless circumcised Timothy not long after the council in Jerusalem. It wasn't to honor the law but to advance the gospel by not overly offending the Jews to whom Timothy would minister.

Food polluted by idols and strangled animal blood no longer seems relevant, but the command to refrain from sexual immorality continues to be a current issue in today's culture. What exactly does that mean? Does it preclude a committed gay couple from enjoying intimacy within a marriage relationship?

The term "sexual immorality" translates the Greek word *pornea,* from which we get our word "pornography". It is vague in specifics, especially considering that those to whom this was originally addressed where Gentiles living in the Roman Empire. Sexual ethics varied widely in that culture and many of the accepted norms were considered sinful by Christians.

If we consider once again Jesus' singular command to love one another and allow that to inform our understanding of sexual morality, then the call here is to use our sexuality only in a truly loving manner. The moral logic of love applied to sexuality is not a free-for-all, but a call to a morally pure sex life. It is using sexuality in ways that express love for ourselves, for others, and for the one who created human sexuality in the beginning.

Whether that morality includes committed LGBTQ partners requires a consideration of the rest of scripture's teachings on the matter . . . . the rest of the story.

9

The Rest of the Story

My view is that ministering to LGBTQ people does not require abandoning the Christian faith but rather focusing more intently on Jesus, the center of our faith. So we've explored how Jesus taught love and showed grace to those discarded by society and rejected by religion. There are a handful of other Bible passages which deal specifically with homosexual behavior that we should also consider.

Richard B. Hays highlights how seldom the Bible addresses homosexuality:

> The Bible hardly ever discussed homosexual behavior. There are perhaps half a dozen brief references to it in all of scripture. In terms of emphasis, it is a minor concern, in contrast, for example, to economic injustice.[1]

It is not just the red letters of Jesus where homosexuality is not addressed. The rest of scripture is virtually silent on the topic.

As a Christian I do have to wrestle with scripture in order to understand it accurately and so that I can apply it to my own life. If all Christians agreed on the interpretation of all passages there would be far fewer denominations and churches. Good, biblical scholars have reconsidered the few passages that specifically address homosexual behavior and have come to new conclusions that honor the integrity of the text while opening the door to a more loving inclusion of LGBTQ people in the church.

I don't believe that such scholars are twisting Bible passages to support their agenda. Rather, within the current cultural context of acceptance, scholars are able to read biblical texts with a new perspective. The Reformed scholar and New Testament professor at Western Seminary in Holland, MI, James Brownson, notes this cultural shift in his excellent book: *Bible, Gender, Sexuality: Reframing the Church's Debate on Same-Sex Relationships.* He writes:

> The church's experience with gay and lesbian people is raising questions that have never been asked before and confronting people with dilemmas they have never faced before. Many of these questions are arising in fresh ways simply because our culture is becoming more direct and frank in its discussion of sexual issues.[2]

Just as the nineteenth-century culture allowed Christians to reconsider the Bible's teaching on slavery and twentieth-century cultural shifts provided context for a new reading of passages about women's roles in society and church, so today's culture enables us to see Bible passages about homosexuality in ways we simply overlooked before.

Reading the scriptures in this new light offers new conclusions, which some label as liberal or even non-Christian. While these interpretations are not traditional, they do honor Christ, maintain the integrity of biblical interpretation, and thus are Christian. Because I am a pastor in a church that honors the Bible and cannot merely dismiss certain passages as being a result Paul's alleged homophobia, I want to summarize valid interpretations of the biblical texts that address homosexuality in ways that open the door for accepting LGBTQ people with Christlike love.

Genesis 19

The story in Genesis 19 about the angels visiting Lot in Sodom, the men of the town surrounding Lot's house and demanding that they be allowed to have sex with these angels, followed by the destruction of Sodom and Gomorrah, has traditionally been used to condemn homosexuality. The word "sodomy" was coined to negatively refer to gay sex.

That's just not a fair reading of that text nor is it consistent with the rest of the Bible's references to Sodom. Even Richard B Hays writes:

> The notorious story of Sodom and Gomorrah—often cited in connection with homosexuality—is actually irrelevant to the topic.[3]

Both here and in a similar account in Judges 19, the sin is rape, not homosexuality.

The real issue is the ultimate lack of hospitality, seeing visitors to their town as merely a means for their own sexual pleasure. Sodom and Gomorrah are icons of evil in the rest of the Bible, examples of godless living and a warning about God's judgement and ultimate destruction of such evil. References to Sodom and Gomorrah read like this:

> "Now this was the sin of your sister Sodom: She and her daughters were arrogant, overfed and unconcerned; they did not help the poor and needy." (Ezekiel 16:49)

Notice that Ezekiel highlights social injustice, not sexual immorality. Matthew Vines writes:

> Sexuality goes unmentioned, both in the Ezekiel passage and in every other Old Testament reference to Sodom following Genesis 19. If Sodom's sin had indeed been same-sex behavior, it's highly unlikely that every written discussion of the city for centuries following its destruction would fail to mention that.[4]

Lack of hospitality, injustice, and a selfish obsession with pleasure is the sin of Sodom and Gomorrah. It is evidenced by their demanding that these angelic beings be handed over as sex toys, but it is also seen in their disregard for the needs of the poor. These twin cities of evil are used throughout the rest of the Old Testament and by Jesus as a warning against the godless evil of neglecting the poor and needy.

To be sure, sexual perversion is mentioned in two of the nine

New Testament references to Sodom and Gomorrah (2 Peter 2:7 and
Jude 7). Jude 7 says that they "gave themselves up to sexual immorality
and perversion." The word "perversion" translates the odd Greek
phrase "going after strange (the Greek word is *hetero*) flesh" and refers
to the fact that these human men of Sodom were hoping to sexually
assault angelic beings.

Given the Old Testament references to social justice and
arrogant materialism that plagued Sodom, the wealthy man in his luxury
car, paid for by exploiting underpaid workers and ignoring the homeless
on his way to church, is guilty of sodomy; not the loving, married gay
couple.

Leviticus

Homosexual acts are condemned in the book of Leviticus
(Leviticus 18:22, 20:13). In some translations the behavior is labeled as
an "abomination." The NIV translation uses the term "detestable." The
Hebrew word is *toevah* and usually is a reference to idolatry. The
Leviticus 20:13 passage calls for the death penalty. It is important to
consider that these commandments were meant to differentiate God's
people from those in Egypt and Canaan (Leviticus 18:3). In those
cultures, lewd homosexual acts were used in idol worship. As Andrew
Marin points out:

> The Holiness Code, another name for Leviticus 17–26,
> defined God's rules to the Israelites in order to maintain
> their holiness as well as their distinctiveness from the
> rest of the world as God's chosen people.[5]

God wants his people to live distinctly for him, not imitating the pagan
lifestyle of the surrounding nations. This is why burning incense and
tattoos were also forbidden for the Israelites.

Seen in this context, prohibitions in Leviticus against same sex
relations are not about sexual orientation, but pagan idolatry. The
commandments addressed sinful perversions that were common in the
ancient cultures surrounding Israel, and God expected more from his
people. Same-sex orientation was not even a consideration in this or

any other Bible passage.

But the real issue with applying Leviticus to people today and to modern relationships is that it was not written for us. It was intended for a specific people in a unique period of history: the Israelites living in the Promised Land. Jesus himself violated the laws in Leviticus by touching a leper and a menstruating, thus unclean, woman. His parable of the Good Samaritan teaches that love overrides law, that violating the Levitical law in order to love a stranger is part of what following Jesus might involve.

Romans 1

Romans 1 is the longest reference in the Bible to homosexuality, and it is only a few verses. The verses are part of Paul's long theological argument for the necessity of grace in every person's life. In building the case that all people have sinned, not just those labeled sinners by religious people, Paul uses unnatural homosexual activity as an example. He writes:

> "God gave them over to shameful lusts. Even their women exchanged natural sexual relations for unnatural ones. In the same way the men also abandoned natural relations with women and were inflamed with lust for one another. Men committed shameful acts with other men, and received in themselves the due penalty for their error." (Romans 1:26-27)

James Brownson highlights that the issues in this passage are lust, shame, and the exchange of what is natural for what is unnatural. He writes that Paul was referring to a "manifestation of self-centered lust, one that is not content with women alone but is driven to ever more exotic and unnatural forms of stimulation in the pursuit of pleasure."[6] This passage addresses sexual orientation only to the extent that unchecked lust causes some to defy their natural orientation to experience some new self-gratifying pleasure. Brownson writes, "we must recognize a gap between what Paul is describing and the modern experience of gay couples seeking marriage."[7]

Brownson makes a compelling case that Paul may be referring to the well-known exploits of the Roman Emperor Gaius Caligula. Caligula reigned not long before Paul wrote Romans and was notorious for his sexual perversions, which included incestuous relations and frequent sexual assaults. One of his victims, a military officer, conspired to murder Caligula, the "due penalty" for his lustful lifestyle. Brownson concludes:

> Gaius Caligula graphically illustrates the reality of which Paul speaks in Romans 1: the movement from idolatry to insatiable lust to every form of depravity, and the violent murderous reprisal that such behavior engenders.[8]

Even if that is not the case, what is certain is that Paul is referring to extreme forms of sexual perversions that follow unrestrained lust and is using it to build a case for his gospel message.

As such, this passage does not address homosexual orientation, the proper expression of such an orientation, or gay marriage. Brownson explains:

> We define the words "gay" and "lesbian," not first of all by behavior, but by sexual orientation; this is not at all the same thing as lust, which is understood as excessive desire. Nor is this merely an artificial verbal distinction; it arises from the actual experience of gay and lesbian persons, experience that went largely unrecognized in the ancient world.[9]

Applying Romans 1 to a committed, loving, gay couple is a misapplication of the text.

Paul is using extreme examples of sin in Romans 1 in order to illustrate in Romans 2:1 that all of us "do the same things." He is making a case for universal sin and the universal need for salvation in Christ. In doing so, he is not referencing something completely unknown to his readers: sexual orientation. This passage can be used to expose the folly of lust in both straight and gay people, but it simply does not address the question of selfless love that exists in healthy homosexual relationships.

Sin is still sin, but homosexual sin is a violation of the same principles of love and commitment that heterosexual sin violates. When the Council in Jerusalem wrote the letter to the church in Antioch telling them to refrain from sexual immorality (Acts 15:23-29), they did not specifically prohibit homosexuality because the new wineskins of the gospel had expanded sufficiently to include all people, even those who were non-Jewish or did not conform to Jewish sexual norms. The command to avoid sexual immorality is a command to use our sexuality with the same overarching principle of selfless love that guides every aspect of our lives.

1 Corinthians 6

This passage in 1 Corinthians 6 has a list of sinful behaviors that indicate that such sinners are not living in the Kingdom of God. It is part of a section where Paul is addressing problems in the early church, specifically lawsuits. Paul writes:

> "Or do you not know that wrongdoers will not inherit the kingdom of God? Do not be deceived: Neither the sexually immoral nor idolaters nor adulterers nor male prostitutes nor homosexual offenders nor thieves nor the greedy nor drunkards nor slanderers nor swindlers will inherit the kingdom of God." (1 Corinthians 6:9-10)

In teaching how Christians should approach lawsuits, Paul explains that it is better to be wronged than to be a wrongdoer. He then lists examples of wrongdoers, warning Christians to not be like them. The message is that they simply must quit suing each other in court.

To understand how this text addresses homosexuality we have to examine the words translated above as "male prostitutes" and "homosexual offenders." These terms are based on two Greek words (*malakoi* and *arsenokoitai*), which have been translated into English with a variety of words based on the theology of the current translators.

Sadly, these two words have often been used as a club to beat up on LGBTQ people. Anti-gay hate speech has used these verses as ammunition along with a theology full of hatred and void of grace. Some twist this passage to falsely teach that LGBTQ people can't be Christians and can't live in the Kingdom of God—in other words, that all gay people are going to hell.

The truth is, both of these Greek words are difficult to translate because scholars aren't sure what they originally meant. What Paul and the Christians in Corinth originally understood by these words is not entirely clear today.

Malakoi is a very common word in ancient Greek literature, and it literally means "soft, feminine, or fine." Some translations use the term "effeminate" for this word. That doesn't necessarily refer to homosexuality, but it might. In ancient literature it also referred to a heterosexual man who cared too much about women. It was not considered manly, in those days, to treat your wife with kindness or favor her with too much attention. It was effeminate to always be talking about feelings, buying jewelry, and putting the toilet seat down.

It also had the nuance of lacking self-control, because it was thought in ancient times that men had more self control than women. After all, women generally cry easier and show their emotions more openly, while manly men don't cry. So macho men in the first century Roman Empire used the term *malakoi* as a put-down for men who were too emotional, too "womanly." These were not gay men, but men that today might be labeled thoughtful or kind.

Corinth was a city full of pagan temples and at least some of its pagan worship involved homosexual acts, often in exchange for money. So in the context of Corinth, *malakoi* may have referred to homosexual prostitutes. It also may have referred to straight men who lacked sexual self-control or men who visited prostitutes, which, in Roman times, were often under-aged boys.

The second word, *arsenokoitai,* is a term that Paul apparently invented. At least, we have no other occurrences of this word in Greek literature from that era. It literally means "male bed," but bed in the sense that we use the term "sleeping together," which refers to more than just sleeping. In later Greek works it does occur and usually refers to economic injustice.

Given the economic nuance of the term, it likely refers to prostitution. Men who use their power or money for sex are included in this list of wrongdoers. This is a huge issue in our "me too" culture today. Even after the sexual revolution and the extreme tolerance of twenty-first century America, we detest those who use power and money to abuse others sexually.

Many scholars believe that these two words are combined to refer to a form of pederasty that was common in the ancient Roman world. Older men either buy or use their power to manipulate young boys to serve them sexually. This was a common practice, well known and accepted in that culture. Paul condemns this evil and uses it as a warning to those who desire to sue fellow believers—they are in company with such perverts.

Over the years Bible translators have struggled to find the right English equivalents for these two Greek words. Among others, it has been translated "abusers of themselves with mankind," "sexual perverts," and "homosexual offenders."

Modern translations of *arsenokoitai* as "practicing homosexuals" or "men who have sex with other men" seems to have more to do with conservative, evangelical politics and sales of NIV Bibles than with good Bible translation. It is loaded with a certain theological interpretation that does not come from good linguistic work but from a homophobic culture that fears what it does not understand. It is unhelpful in determining what the original text is really communicating.

These words are condemning abusive, homosexual sin, not homosexual orientation or loving homosexual expressions. Like all the others sins listed in this passage (including heterosexual), the focus is to avoid abusing and using other people for your own selfish gain, whether that is sexually, financially, or through civil lawsuits. And the point is to deter Christians from abusing each other through civil lawsuits.

Eugene Peterson gets to the heart of this list and these particular words in his Message translation:

> "Don't you realize that this is not the way to live? Unjust people who don't care about God will not be joining in his kingdom. Those who use and abuse each other, use and abuse sex, use and abuse the earth and everything in it, don't qualify as citizens in God's kingdom." (1 Corinthians 6:9-10, from *The Message: The Bible in Contemporary Language*.)

1 Timothy 1:9-10

In Paul's first letter to Timothy, called 1 Timothy in the Bible, he is instructing the younger pastor how to lead and teach the church. Paul begins by encouraging Timothy to stand firm against those who are teaching false doctrines in the church, teachings that contradict love and sincere faith (1 Timothy 1:5).

Paul says that the law is good only when used properly, when it reveals sin in order to lead sinners to the glorious gospel. As in 1 Corinthians 6, Paul then lists certain sinners as examples of those in need of the law:

> "We also know that the law is made not for the righteous but for lawbreakers and rebels, the ungodly and sinful, the unholy and irreligious, for those who kill their fathers or mothers, for murderers, for the sexually immoral and perverts, for slave traders and liars and perjurers." (1 Timothy 1:9-10)

The word translated "perverts" is the Greek word *arsenokoitai,* the word Paul invented in 1 Corinthians 6 to condemn the abusive practice of child prostitution in that culture. The very next word in the text is "slave traders" which only strengthens the argument that *arsenokoitai* was a reference to prostitution, which, both then and now, is related to sex trafficking.

The newest NIV Bible version has altered its translation to "those practicing homosexuality." Again, this is an unfortunate translation that seems based more on market pressures than on good scholarship.

There is a vast difference between two gay men committed to a loving marriage and a pedophile who slithers into a crowded city brothel to buy sex from a twelve-year-old slave boy. To equate the two, to take a passage intended to condemn the vile abuse of a minor child and twist it to pass judgment on a love-based relationship where partners care about each other's well-being, is a terrible perversion of the text. Such twisting of scripture is, oddly enough, the very thing Paul is warning Timothy against in this passage.

This text can be used to address the terrible problem of sex trafficking in the world, but simply does not speak to the topic of loving, homosexual relationships. In fact, all of the passages in the Bible traditionally used to denounce homosexuality are condemning lust and do not address homosexual orientation or heathy gay relationships.

A Reasonable Doubt

This is not a black and white issue as some conservative Christians believe. There are literally hundreds of books written by Christian scholars that articulate an affirming theology of homosexuality, using scripture to teach an acceptance of what was once unacceptable. If we claim that only a plain and simple reading of the Bible is legitimate, that any scholarly work to better define biblical texts is misleading, then we would also mire the church in racism and sexism, affirming the first-century slavery of the Roman world instead of embracing the equal rights built on the moral logic of biblical love. I cannot condemn my gay brothers and sisters because of a misreading of several scriptures anymore than I can embrace the ownership of slaves or the degrading of women.

My fear is that most Christians have scarcely even read these passages, let alone considered their original meaning in the historical context to which they were written.

Not all Christians will accept the exegetical work behind these conclusions, but if there is some doubt about how to interpret these very sparse verses that specifically address homosexual behavior, then shouldn't we err on the side of grace and assume a posture of love?

I cannot definitively say that these new ways of understanding these scriptures are absolutely the only and correct way, but they do make sense. They are reasonable. Whatever exegetical doubts I might have are overshadowed by the clear command by Jesus to love one another. Just as a reasonable doubt in the courts requires a jury to free the accused, so a reasonable doubt about scripture's teaching on homosexuality requires us to freely accept and openly love LGBTQ persons.

A hateful, judgmental, condemning interpretation of a text cannot be correct because it does not align with the central theme of

Jesus' ministry. Fresh understandings of Bible texts dealing with slavery, women's rights, and divorce brought a completely new understanding to the church and opened the way for more loving inclusion. A careful re-examination of these texts should also open the door for welcoming LGBTQ people into our lives and loving inclusion within our churches.

10

A Glass of Wine at a Gay Wedding

I wasn't sure that I wanted to write this chapter because it addresses a problem that should no longer exist. Before I had seriously read and examined the five or six texts traditionally used to condemn homosexuality, before I came to a better understanding of those passages in light of the entire narrative of the Bible, the central idea in this chapter helped me accept and love LGBTQ people. So it may help those who refuse to acknowledge a new and more accepting way of interpreting these Bible verses do the same.

Sometimes you need to drink a glass of wine and allow others that same liberty without judgement.

The Apostle Paul had a young apprentice named Timothy. Timothy learned how to be a pastor from Paul and eventually was stationed as a pastor in the city of Ephesus. The water in Ephesus was different from the water in his hometown of Lystra, and apparently it was affecting Timothy's health. Paul wrote Timothy several encouraging letters that are contained in the New Testament. The first of these letters, called 1 Timothy, has some advice we all need to apply at times:

> "Stop drinking only water, and use a little wine because of your stomach and your frequent illnesses." (1 Timothy 5:23)

Timothy's problem was what used to be called "skitters," a folksy way of speaking about diarrhea. Skitters is a real problem when you travel in India with an American stomach. My brother went with me once and got a bad case of skitters. Fortunately for him, my niece was along and had remembered anti-diarrheal medicine. Unfortunately, she mistook her allergy medicine for the anti-diarrheal medicine. So my brother's nose wasn't running, but everything else was. This was Timothy's problem and it was getting in the way of his ministry.

Paul tells Timothy to quit drinking water all the time; have a glass of wine. Sometimes you have to drink wine because your stomach just can't handle the local water.

The Need for Wine

Why was this command even necessary? Why was Timothy only drinking water and avoiding wine?

It might have been because of Paul's letter to the church in Ephesus, where he taught:

"Do not get drunk on wine, which leads to debauchery.
Instead, be filled with the Spirit." (Ephesians 5:18)

Even in the letter of 1 Timothy, Paul warns of indulging in too much wine:

"In the same way, deacons are to be worthy of respect, sincere, not indulging in much wine." (1 Timothy 3:8)

Timothy probably knew about the passage in Romans which read:

"Do not destroy the work of God for the sake of food. All food is clean, but it is wrong for a person to eat anything that causes someone else to stumble. It is better not to eat meat or drink wine or to do anything else that will cause your brother or sister to fall." (Romans 14:20-21)

Given all these warnings, perhaps Timothy decided it was better to abstain completely from drinking wine.

There are a lot of warnings about alcohol abuse in the New Testament. Even today, many Christians choose to abstain from any alcohol because of how it can ruin people's lives or affect the faith of others. Because he was a young pastor and didn't want his witness for Christ compromised, Timothy chose to drink only water and avoid alcohol altogether.

And Paul tells him, commands him really, to stop.

Paul's instruction is, "Use a little wine."

This isn't permission to polish off the whole bottle and get smashed. Paul wants Timothy to realize that he has a weak stomach, and that sometimes we need to make allowances for our own weakness. Because of your stomach and your frequent skitters, use a little wine.

I have literally taken this advice. There were times overseas where I order a beer because I believed it was the safest thing for my digestive system. Even those times when I ordered a cold beer because the air was steaming hot, it was because of my weakness in hot climates, a concession to my thirst.

It is too easy for Christians, pastors like me especially, to become overly concerned about things like alcohol. Paul is encouraging Timothy, and all of us, to not be legalistic about alcohol, to quit being judgmental or allow the judgementalism of others to dictate our behavior.

The Message translation of 1 Timothy 5:23 highlights this concern about judgementalism:

> "And don't worry too much about what the critics will say. Go ahead and drink a little wine, for instance; it's good for your digestion, good medicine for what ails you." (1 Timothy 5:23, from *The Message: The Bible in Contemporary Language*)

That advice from Paul to Timothy is based on both the goodness of creation and the freedom we have as Christians to enjoy that goodness.

There is another principle at work here that might not be as obvious, but might change the way we view and treat others.

The Principle of Concession

I call this The Principle of Concession, or The Principle of a Little Wine. A concession is granting someone an exception, making an allowance for them based on their unique situation. We don't expect our buddy in a wheelchair to help us roof our house, our four-year-old to drive himself to preschool, or a parent with dementia to remember our birthday. Life is never perfect and so you make do, you compromise, you make an allowance for a weak stomach.

Timothy had been avoiding wine despite his recurring skitters. When I was first a pastor I was sensitive to being judged for being young. I was discreet when I enjoyed a beer because I didn't want to be accused of being a drunk or allow alcohol to interfere with my ministry. I imagine Timothy had the same concerns and was being overly sensitive.

While drinking wine may have its hazards, it is a concession to Timothy's weakness, his inability to function without a little wine. It is because of his weak stomach, his frequent illness, that he needs to become a wine-drinking young pastor.

In the Garden of Eden, in the perfect state of creation before sin polluted everything, a person could drink water from any river, lake, or waterfall without worrying about bacteria. Adam and Eve did not need to filter or boil their water. But then sin ruined creation to its very core. The water meant to strengthen our bodies sometimes destroys them instead. In a world with harmful micro-organisms, use a little wine.

The Principle of Concession takes into account the devastating effects of sin and how it wreaks havoc on our broken souls and frail bodies. It meet us at our point of weakness and offers specific help. It admits that in this lifetime perfection is out of reach but, with mercy, progress is possible.

The Bible teaches that we are all sinners, every one of us in need of grace. "For all have sinned and fall short of the glory of God." (Romans 3:23). The Principle of Concession is that God shows all of us grace, that while we were still sinners, Christ died for us.

The Principle of Concession is what prompted the incarnation of Jesus. Every Christmas we celebrate the story of God not waiting for us to rise up to his level of perfection and holiness, but rather that he, in Christ, descended to our level of broken humanity. He emptied himself and lived among us as a servant. He didn't just come to earth and live in an isolated palace, he humbled himself enough to mingle with sinners, to seek and to save the lost, the least, the overlooked, and despised.

The Principle of Concession defined the life and mission of Jesus.

Philippians 2 teaches that it should define those who follow Jesus as well:

> "Your attitude should be the same as that of Christ Jesus: Who, being in very nature God, did not consider equality with God something to be grasped, but made himself nothing . . ." (Philippians 2:5-7)

We are called to approach others with that same humility and offer the same grace to others that we ourselves have received in Christ. We are to make concessions for the brokenness, the weakness, and the inherent flaws in ourselves and in others. Churches should not be places where people hide their problems and put on masks of perfection, but communities where grace is offered to those wounded by life.

Use a little wine, because in a broken world, sometimes the water is polluted and will eventually kill you.

And, allow others, even your young pastor, to drink a little wine, because he has a weak stomach. Don't judge or condemn him for his weakness. Natives of Ephesus, who could drink the water without trouble, wondered what was wrong with Timothy. Instead of judging, they needed to give him a break and let him have his glass of wine.

This offering of grace to others is exactly what Paul teaches Christians to do in the book of Ephesians:

> "Be completely humble and gentle; be patient, bearing with one another in love." (Ephesians 4:2)

As Christ bears with us while we stumble along the way of following him, so we are to offer grace to others. Let them drink a little wine in order to live their best life in Ephesus.

Wine for Young Widows

This principle is applied not just to drinking wine, but in at least two other ways just in the book of 1 Timothy.

Paul writes to Timothy regarding young widows in the church. With a shorter life expectancy in the first century and the fact that women often outlive men, there were far more young widows than there are today. Paul counsels Timothy to make a list of elderly widows that needed to be cared for by the church, but adds:

> "As for younger widows, do not put them on such a list. For when their sensual desires overcome their dedication to Christ, they want to marry. . . So I counsel younger widows to marry, to have children, to manage their homes and to give the enemy no opportunity for slander." (1 Timothy 5:11-14)

Paul teaches that it is better for older widows to remain single, to devote themselves to prayer, hospitality, and helping those in need. While in some ways it may be better for young widows to do the same, given the strength of their sensual desires, Paul says that they should get married. It is a concession to their natural humanity, their youthful hormones, and their need for intimacy. Not everyone can live alone.

This is very similar to the advice Paul offers to the church in Corinth:

> "Now for the matters you wrote about: It is good for a man not to marry. But since there is so much immorality, each man should have his own wife, and each woman her own husband. . . because of your lack of self-control. I say this as a concession, not as a command. I wish that all men were as I am. But each man has his own gift from God; one has this gift, another has that. Now to the unmarried and the widows I say: It is good for them to stay unmarried, as I am. But if they cannot control themselves, they should marry, for it is better to marry than to burn with passion." (1 Corinthians 7:1-9)

Paul is single, but realizes that not everyone has this gift of singleness. So as a concession to our humanity with its passions and struggles for self-control, we should get married and enjoy that permanent, loving, relationship where intimacy can be safely experienced.

Certainly there are people, like Paul, who have the gift of singleness. For the rest of us, there is marriage. It is, at least in part, a concession to our human condition—the weakness of our wills.

And yet, marriage is a thing of beauty, a relationship that models love and brings glory to God. Marriage is a good thing in a broken world. Marriage, while a concession to our nearly uncontrollable passions, is also redeemed by God and used for his purposes.

Wine for Slaves

There is another concession in 1 Timothy, one that might shock modern readers. Like a number of letters in the New Testament, 1 Timothy regulates slavery. Historically, in America and in other countries, the Bible was used both to support and to end slavery.

Those who used the Bible to support slavery did not understand the moral logic of love that undergirds the Bible. They failed to see the Principle of Concession behind New Testament commands to slave owners and to Christian slaves. The Bible does not condone slavery; God created all people for freedom. There were no slaves in the Garden of Eden—there will be no slaves in the New Heaven and the New Earth.

But there are slaves in the in-between time, throughout human history.

And the Bible, including 1 Timothy, gives instructions for slaves on how to live out their faith in this broken world where freedom may never be experienced by some people:

> "All who are under the yoke of slavery should consider their masters worthy of full respect, so that God's name and our teaching may not be slandered." (1 Timothy 6:1)

Similar commands are found in Ephesians 6:5-9, which also includes teachings for masters to treat their slaves with kindness and justice.

In today's world, we would love to re-write those verses to say, "Masters, free your slaves just as in Christ Jesus you have been freed from your sin. No child of God should ever own another human being." But that is not what it says. It is a concession, commands given in a Roman world where as much as one-third of the human beings were slaves of some kind: treat them fairly, do not threaten them. This isn't condoning slavery; it is a concession to the broken world in which we live.

Yes, Jesus changes everything.

But not all at once.

Yes, Jesus sets us free! But some are still living in bondage.

Many Christians limp into heaven. Some crawl after a lifetime of being beaten down by the pain and injustice of this world. Others are carried in because they are too wounded and wrecked by the sin and destruction in this world.

Passages that regulate slavery are not the ideal; the ideal will be in the New Heaven and the New Earth, where all nations and tribes gather as one to worship our Lord in complete harmony.

These are concessions to the cruelty of this broken world.

Wine for Divorce and Remarriage

Some concessions, like dealing with divorce, are more complicated for Bible-believing Christians. A few years ago at our church I looked up at our stage during worship and realized that almost every person leading worship that day had been or was going through a divorce. There was a time in church history, not very long ago, when divorced people would have been asked to not play the piano or lead the singing. And yet, on a given Sunday, there were six people in my conservative, Bible-believing church leading worship despite the fact that they had all been divorced.

The Bible's teaching on divorce is pretty clear. Jesus, in the Sermon on the Mount, taught:

> "It has been said, 'Anyone who divorces his wife must give her a certificate of divorce.' But I tell you that anyone who divorces his wife, except for marital unfaithfulness, causes her to become an adulteress, and anyone who marries the divorced woman commits adultery." (Matthew 5:31-32)

So was our piano player at church committing adultery by marrying a divorced man, and allowing him to marry her after her divorce?

Paul, commenting on Jesus, trying to apply this ethic to the early church, teaches:

> "To the married I give this command (not I, but the Lord): A wife must not separate from her husband. But if she does, she must remain unmarried or else be reconciled to her husband. And a husband must not divorce his wife." (1 Corinthians 7:10-11)

There doesn't seem to be a lot of wiggle room in these passages. Divorce and remarriage is not God's best for us.

Divorce has, in one way or another, effected almost every family in America. One of my life's saddest days was helping my brother move his stuff out of his house, which had just been sold to settle his divorce. After a long day of work we sat on the porch of his tiny duplex and shared a beer in the dark. We didn't say much because there wasn't much worth saying. We both put on our game face, but it was depressing. Divorce hurts.

Divorce isn't God's best for his children. God loves us. He doesn't wish that pain on anyone.

Divorce itself is a concession to our collective human sinfulness. There are people who are impossible to be married to. There are couples who should never have gotten married. There are abusive people who ruin marriages and there are events that destroy the trust needed to remain married.

Divorce is always a concession. It is never the optimal. No one on their wedding day says, "This is great! I can't wait for the divorce."

Marriage is meant to be permanent. Divorce is a concession—sometimes the best option for a ruined marriage.

So is remarriage after divorce.

There is not a verse in the Bible that says, "After three years you can get remarried." Or, "If he was a scum, you are free to remarry."

And yet, in the church, we have come to realize that divorced people can get remarried, that those who have gone through the pain of divorce are still loved by God, are no more or less sinners than those of us who have not been divorced.

What we have done is watch Jesus, who met a woman at a well who was living with a man and had been divorced five times. Jesus offers her grace, acceptance, love, and forgiveness. He offers her the living water of a fresh start (John 4:4-26).

There is not a single verse to lean on, but rather the entire theme of the Bible that says we are all sinners, that no sin is greater than another, and that grace can restore us to righteousness in Christ. It is the moral logic of love that allows a conservative church like mine, a church that holds to the Bible as God's word, to have divorced people leading worship and rejoice in the grace that has restored their lives from pain back to joy.

One of the greatest days of my life was a Sunday afternoon a few years later when that same brother married a woman who loved him, adored his kids, and brought wholeness back to his life. Their relationship is a picture of grace—God's grace that mends what was broken.

By loving divorced people, by including them in the leadership of the church, we are not saying that we don't believe in marriage, that we think divorce is okay, that divorce is no big deal. We are, rather, saying that sometime skitters happens, and use a little wine because of your weakness and because this harsh world leaves us all wounded in one way or another.

Most churches have applied the principle of concession to this area of life. We love divorced people; we even see a picture of God's grace in a second marriage. While we continue to believe that God's best plan for all marriages is that they are permanent, joy producing, life-long relationships of faithful love, we allow for divorce and remarriage within our church community.

When marriages do break we don't worsen their situation with a barrage of condemnation and judgement. Christians have learned to extend grace and offer love to our divorced brothers and sisters. This has made all of us more honest sinners and more humble saints.

Wine for Our Gay Friends

Even if you still consider homosexuality to be a sin, the Principle of Concession allows you to accept, support, and love LGBTQ persons, and even to support gay marriage as a concession to the many destructive alternatives.

Whether people are born with homosexual orientation or develop it early in life, it clearly is not a willful choice. Tony Campolo writes:

> While nobody knows what causes a homosexual orientation, we *do* know that people don't choose to be homosexuals. I have met a number of Christian men who are gay, who talk about having walked the floor at night, crying out to God for deliverance, and their sexual orientation has not changed.[1]

If sexual orientation or feeling transgender was merely a personal, moral choice, then people could will themselves to change. Even extensive therapy, in almost all cases, has done little to alter such inner convictions.

Should we not treat LGBTQ people with the same kindness we offer to all? If we offer mercy to the divorced despite the clear teaching against it in the Bible, shouldn't we also offer a similar grace to LGBTQ people? You can still maintain that this is not God's best, not the ideal for any human being, but as a concession to our collective brokenness, you can offer grace and extend love. You can concede that gay marriage is a far better alternative than either a life of promiscuous sexual encounters or a life of isolated loneliness.

As the Principle of Concession guides your response to LGBTQ persons, it does not require a change in your own theology or ethics anymore than loving and accepting divorced people changes your view of marriage. You are simply acknowledging that, in a world stained by sin where all of us are affected by that sin in different ways, some people end up with a unique sexual orientation or identity.

Bible-believing Christians consider the big picture of salvation throughout the Bible's narrative. In the perfection of the Garden of

Eden, God created a man and a woman, they were married, naked and unashamed. They were completely comfortable with who they were in this sinless paradise.

And at the end of the Bible's narrative we see paradise restored. Jesus explains that there won't even be marriage in heaven (Matthew 22:30). It seems likely that gender itself either won't exist or won't be important in heaven—our reproductive organs aren't going to be needed for procreation. We will be changed. We don't know how exactly, but it will be glorious and heavenly. We will all be restored and finally see ourselves and each other as we were meant to be. The shackles of sin and all of the ruin it causes to our psyches, our relationships, our spiritual life, and our physical bodies—even down to our DNA, will be removed and replaced with heavenly perfection.

But for now we live in the in-between.

In this world there are people who are born with same-sex attraction. All of the scientific evidence points to that reality. There are people who have gender dysphoria, who feel like they aren't the gender that they were biologically assigned at birth.

As Christians, we say, "God doesn't make mistakes."

And yet, here we all are, all of us stained by sin, marred in various ways so that sometimes in Ephesus you need to drink a little wine to get by with a weak stomach.

Christians must offer the grace to LGBTQ people that Paul and the church in Ephesus offered to Timothy. None of us are perfect; all of us require gracious concessions to accommodate our flaws and our humanity. We must accept LGBTQ people with love if we are to be faithful to the Jesus we claim to follow.

Accepting Gay Marriage

While there are some people, gay and straight, who have the gift of celibacy like the Apostle Paul, it seems that the vast majority of us crave the intimacy and companionship that comes from having a life partner, a sexual partner. In a world where hormones can rage, the biblical advice is that it is better to marry than to burn with passion. It is better to find real intimacy in a committed marriage than to jump from bed to bed looking for something to quench your desires.

Paul's counsel to the Christians in Corinth is certainly a concession to straight people, and can easily be applied to LGBTQ people as well:

> "Now to the unmarried and the widows I say: It is good for them to stay unmarried, as I am. But if they cannot control themselves, they should marry, for it is better to marry than to burn with passion." (1 Corinthians 7:8-9)

Lifelong celibacy is a gift, not a mandate imposed on others, not even for religious purposes. Paul tells Timothy that a group of false teachers who forbid marriage are "hypocritical liars, whose consciences have been seared as with a hot iron." (1 Timothy 4:2).

Here's how the Principle of Concession works for most pastors: A couple comes to me and wants me to do their wedding. They are living together. Our church doesn't believe that living together and being sexually intimate before marriage is the right way for couples to move toward marriage. We have even, traditionally, labeled this: "living in sin." I've explained to couples that, statistically, living together before marriage might seem like a good test run but actually increases the odds of the marriage ending in divorce.

I have met a few pastors who insist that couples live apart for a period of time prior to the wedding. But most of us realize that such an arrangement isn't ideal, that the couple will simply go down the street to another pastor or find a judge to perform the ceremony. So we do the wedding, realizing that this is not the ideal situation, but that it is the best way forward.

I have done countless weddings like this. No one has accused me of selling out my faith or denying my ordination vows. And yet we have not extended that same grace to gay couples wishing to marry.

You can maintain that it is not the ideal. You can insist that God's plan was for one man and one woman to be united in marriage. But just as divorce adds new variables into that equation, so homosexual orientation requires a concession to find the best path forward.

I don't have a Bible verse that specifically says, "Let's welcome gay people as fellow sinners." anymore than I have a Bible verse that tells us to welcome divorced people as fellow sinners. The moral logic of love, the narrative flow of the Bible's redemptive history, brings us to the conclusion of showing grace and love to all, including LGBTQ people.

Even if you reject the careful biblical analysis summarized in the previous chapter, by applying the Principle of Concession, offering the same love, grace, and mercy that has been offered to us in Christ, you can and should accept LGBTQ people and welcome them into your life and into the fellowship of your church. You can accept that same-sex marriage may be the best path forward for some, a concession not unlike all marriages. And that some of these marriages might also be redeemed by God and used for his purposes.

We are all works in progress, broken in various ways by the sin that will someday be nothing but a memory. Until that day, let's drink a little wine. And let's allow others that same liberty.

11

My Jesus is Your Jesus

I believe that Jesus was a real person, that he was born to Mary and Joseph in a miraculous conception, that he lived the life chronicled in the four gospels, died on a Roman cross, was buried in a borrowed tomb, and rose again on the Sunday we now call Easter. I believe that the historic Jesus is the biblical Jesus and that he is truly the savior of the world. Jesus is the center of the Christian faith and the center of mine.

Jesus is not a religious construct that someone can mold into an image convenient to their cause. There is a recorded history of Jesus, words and actions captured in four nuanced accounts. In other words, there is no "my Jesus" because my Jesus is your Jesus.

And your Jesus loves gays.

I also believe that the Bible, as God's word, should form our understanding and guide our faith, not the opposite. Unless we try to understand the biblical message, setting aside our own biases and distortions, even allowing the Bible to override centuries of church dogma and tradition, then the text can't truly inform or form us. If the Bible is God's revelation of himself, revealing the relationship he desires with us and the life he calls us to live; in other words, if it is God's truth, then we need to submit to it as our authority for life.

I grew up reading the Bible and hearing it preached with the anti-gay bias that prevailed in American culture. Gay people were mocked in our culture and condemned in our churches. I never heard a careful examination of the scriptures used to come to such conclusions in any of the churches I attended.

79

Fortunately our culture has changed, which has also allowed many Christian churches to rethink the Bible's teaching on homosexuality. With the blinders of prejudice removed, many of us have come to see the Bible's teaching as accepting of LGBTQ people and encouraging them to join the ranks of lepers, tax collectors, adulteresses, and pastors who follow Jesus in the adventure of abundant living.

Be The Church

Love is what people see or fail to see when they encounter Christian people and the local church. If we fail to offer the love of Jesus then no one will accept the truth of Jesus. I have spent my entire life serving within the local church and I love it. I want us to be faithful to the command to love one another, to love gays like our Jesus loves gays.

No one will accept the love of Jesus if they can't experience that love in his people. If those who claim to be followers of Jesus don't love LGBTQ people, then how can we tell them that Jesus loves them; and why would they believe that message?

Love is visible spirituality. It is our greatest and only witness.

When gay couples come into our churches, let's welcome them without condition. When our loved one finally trusts us enough to reveal their true sexual identity, let's celebrate the unique way that God created them. Let's help them discover that LGBTQ people who commit to each other in marriage (or as close to marriage as is legally permissible) are as beautiful an expression of love as any married straight couple. Let's encourage them to see their lives as a gift from God and help them glorify God in their own unique way.

Most LGBTQ people, especially those who grew up in Christian families, feel condemned by God because the church has condemned their sexual orientation. Meanwhile Christians are tempted to think of themselves as morally superior to those outside the church, especially those who don't conform to traditional Christian norms.

I find this parable by Jesus to be a humbling wake-up call:

"To some who were confident of their own righteousness and looked down on everyone else, Jesus told this parable: "Two men went up to the temple to pray, one a Pharisee and the other a tax collector. The Pharisee stood by himself and prayed: 'God, I thank you that I am not like other people—robbers, evildoers, adulterers—or even like this tax collector. I fast twice a week and give a tenth of all I get.'

But the tax collector stood at a distance. He would not even look up to heaven, but beat his breast and said, 'God, have mercy on me, a sinner.'

I tell you that this man, rather than the other, went home justified before God. For all those who exalt themselves will be humbled, and those who humble themselves will be exalted." (Luke 18:9-14)

LGBTQ people, like tax collectors of old, have been humbled by society's rejection of them. They are the ones who cry out for mercy, while the guardians of religion cling to their outdated rules and claim moral superiority. Jesus came to reclaim the right to offer mercy to the humble, to bypass, if necessary, the religion of the day in order to express his love for all.

That Jesus loves gays.

Any choice to belittle, mock, hate or exclude LGBTQ people is a choice to veer away from the path Jesus walked, the path he calls us to follow.

Your Jesus loves gays. He embraces them with open arms and welcomes them to his table. The question remaining is whether or not you will join him.

12

My Kids Are Your Kids

The truth is we aren't going to meet Freddy Mercury because he has already met Jesus. Instead, we need to decide how to respond to the gay person who is our fifteen-year-old niece, the nineteen-year-old who grew up in our church, or our best friend from high school.

Jesus said that what you do for the least of those in need, you are really doing to him, whether you ignore those needs or respond with compassion (Matthew 25:40). When someone, especially a young person, reveals to you that they are gay, they are exposing one of the most intimate aspects of their lives. In a world that defaults to mocking and despising anyone different, it is critical that those who follow Jesus respond with love to anyone being so vulnerable and honest. We must accept them with love and kindness if we have anything of the true Jesus in us. And when we love those who are struggling with life, doubt, rejection, fear, or their own sin, Jesus says it will be as if we are loving him.

John picks up this truth: "No one has ever seen God; but if we love one another, God lives in us and his love is made complete in us." (1 John 4:12). Isn't that our wish?

Truth in Love

I've been accused of no longer being able to view this issue objectively because I have gay kids, that my theology is now skewed by my love for those closest to me.

That is absolutely true.

When the Bible uses the term "speaking the truth in love" (Ephesians 4:15), isn't it requiring us to evaluate truth through the experience of our love? The warm, loving relationships that establish the Kingdom of God are not constructed from cold, hard truths. Receiving and giving truth should always be done through the experience of genuine love.

I cannot read Bible passages or books about homosexuality without thinking about some of the people I most love in this world. My viewpoint is colored by that love. These are not academic truths in a laboratory; these are the lives of my own children.

Whether you like it or not, the truth is that my kids are your kids.

Experts estimate that about five percent of the population currently identifies as LGBTQ. If there are a hundred people in your family tree, there are probably about five LGBTQ relatives hiding somewhere in the branches. Whether they ever come out and share who they really are to you will depend on how you think about and discuss LGBTQ issues and people. They'll wait until they believe you are a safe confidant before trusting you with one of their most intimate truths.

What will most likely change your mind is your heart. When someone you love tells you they are gay, you will be forced to decide whether you will love that person with the loving abandon that God has offered you, or whether you will withhold that love until that person meets some predetermined criteria. If that criteria is for them to become straight then you have chosen to forfeit that relationship permanently.

If you choose to love as Jesus has loved you and has clearly called you to love others, you become a conduit for God's love to that person. They will know that Jesus loves them because you love them.

I have quoted from a book called *Homosexuality in the Church: Both Sides of the Debate*. It has thirteen chapters, each written by a different expert. Some argue for and others against the full acceptance of LGBTQ people in the church. These are intelligent scholars with impressive credentials, each building a solid case that leads to opposing conclusions. I'm not sure how many people will change their positions based on a book like that, or a book like this.

It will be love that opens your eyes to a greater depth and width of God's love. Your love for that child, sister, or friend will open your eyes to Bible passages that might at first seem to condemn the person, but turn out to only condemn the sin, the same sin that dwells within us all. Your love for a gay person will bring you to the point where you realize the truth: your Jesus loves gays.

See the Real Jesus

My hope in writing this is to encourage those who follow Jesus and honor his teaching to re-consider how to relate to LGBTQ people in a more Christlike manner. Following Jesus might mean changing your attitudes and actions; it will require that you abandon your prejudices and biases in favor of sacrificial love. You may end up being labeled a friend of sinners, but you will be in good company.

But I also want to offer a clear picture of Jesus as the one who loves and accepts you as a gay person. The world may have been cruel to you and religious people may have hurled Bible verses at you that distorted God as hateful, who condemns LGBTQ people without exception. I am telling you that is not the God of the Bible, not the witness of Jesus Christ. As a pastor in a Christian church, it hurts my heart to think of the way some Christians and Christian churches have reacted to those who come out as gay. In their most vulnerable state, instead of experiencing love, they encountered hatred.

I am deeply sorry and ashamed that those who follow Christ did not act more like him.

Look past the failures of the church and see Jesus. Receive his embrace of love, the light yoke of his acceptance. You need it as much as I do—all of our souls are weary without his help.

The Jesus who loves gays loves you!

Be The Real Jesus

Sadly, most LGBTQ people will tell that the two places they feel most judged are at church and with their religious relatives. That's ironic, because we follow Jesus who told us not to judge or we ourselves will be judged in the same way (Matthew 7:1), who held up the humble sinner as an example against the self-righteous religious person (Luke

18:14), who never turned his back on a person in need of his love and mercy.

If Jesus loves gays, then why in the world would we want to stand between him and the people he loves?

Isn't it time for those of us who follow Jesus to do the same?

I'm still sitting in my home office in a house full of gay teens. I don't have all the details of a complex theology ironed out, but I know beyond a doubt that my Jesus loves gays. In a sense, that really does explain everything.

Notes

Chapter 5

1. Scot McKnight, *The Jesus Creed: Loving God, Loving Others* (Brewster, MA: Paraclete Press, 2004), 53.
2. McKnight, *The Jesus Creed*, 53.
3. McKnight, *The Jesus Creed*, 57.

Chapter 6

1. James V. Brownson, *Bible, Gender, and Sexuality: Reframing the Church's Debate on Same-Sex Relationships* (Grand Rapids, MI: Eerdmans, 2013), page 172.

Chapter 7

1. Richard B. Hays, "Awaiting the Redemption of Our Bodies," in *Homosexuality in The Church: Both Sides of the Debate* (Louisville, KY: Westminster John Knox Press, 1994), page 11.

Chapter 8

1. Jeffrey S. Siker, "Homosexual Christians, the Bible, and Gentile Inclusion: Confessions of a Repenting Heterosexist," in *Homosexuality in The Church: Both Sides of the Debate* (Louisville, KY: Westminster John Knox Press, 1994), page 187.
2. Jeffrey S. Siker, "Homosexual Christians, the Bible, and Gentile Inclusion," page 188.

Chapter 9

1. Richard B. Hays, "Awaiting the Redemption of Our Bodies," page 5.
2. James V. Brownson, *Bible, Gender, and Sexuality*, page 11.
3. Richard B. Hays, "Awaiting the Redemption of Our Bodies," page 5.
4. Matthew Vines, *God and the Gay Christian: The Biblical Case in Support of Same-Sex Relationships* (New York: Convergent Books, 2014), page 64.
5. Andrew Marin, *Love is An Orientation: Elevating the Conversation with the Gay Community* (Downer's Grove, IL: InterVarsity Press, 2009), page 122.
6. Brownson, *Bible, Gender, Sexuality*, 156.
7. Brownson, *Bible, Gender, Sexuality*, 169.
8. Brownson, *Bible, Gender, Sexuality*, 157.
9. Brownson, *Bible, Gender, Sexuality*, 172.

Chapter 10

1. Shane Claiborne and Tony Campolo, *Red Letter Revolution: What if Jesus Really Meant What He Said?* (Nashville, TN: Thomas Nelson, 2012), page 128.

Index of Scripture References

R obert Williams lives west of the Rockies with his wife and two youngest children. He pastors a hundred kind souls in a church in the heart of his small town and is involved in a ministry that cares for orphans and lepers in rural India. He is the graduate of two well-known theological seminaries (M.Div, D.Min) and is ordained in a protestant denomination.

Made in the USA
Monee, IL
18 June 2021